S0-AQK-347

PRACTICAL GARDENING

Member Ideas

NATIONAL HOME
GARDENING CLUB

Minnetonka, Minnesota

Practical Gardening—Member Ideas

Mike Vail
Vice President,
Product & Business Development

Tom Carpenter
Director of Book Development

Dan Kennedy
Book Production Manager

Michele Teigen
Senior Book Development Coordinator

Gina Germ
Becky Fitch
Photo Editors

Paul Peterson
Editor

Zachary Marell
Book Design & Production

1 2 3 4 5 / 05 04 03 02 01
ISBN 1-58159-082-2

National Home Gardening Club
12301 Whitewater Drive
Minnetonka, MN 55343
www.gardeningclub.com

PHOTO CREDITS

John Greggor/Coldsnap Photography
David Cavagnaro/NHGC Archive
Michael Landis/NHGC Archive
Chuck Crandall and Barbara Crandall
Crandall/NHGC Archive
David Brus/NHGC Archive
John Mowers/NHGC Archive
Bill Adams
Saxon Holt
©Ted Levin/Animals, Animals p. 68

ILLUSTATORS

Bill Reynolds
Bryan Liedahl
Nancy Wirsig McLure/Hand-to-Mouse Arts

The National Home Gardening Club proudly presents this special book which includes some personal favorite recipes of your fellow Members. Each recipe has been screened by a cooking professional and edited for clarity. However, we are not able to kitchen-test these recipes and cannot guarantee their outcome, or your safety in their preparation or consumption.

CONTENTS

NATIONAL HOME
GARDENING CLUB

INTRODUCTION

Everybody can find time for some Practical Gardening!

We live in busy times. It doesn't seem to matter who you are, what stage of life you're at, where you live, what your job is or what your responsibilities are: It's always a challenge to find time to do the things we love to do.

And of course, as a National Home Gardening Club member, gardening is one of those pastimes you're always needing to find time for. So when you do find a few minutes or (almost miraculously) a few hours to spend gardening, you want the time to be fun; but your work also needs to be efficient and show some results.

That's what this book, **Practical Gardening,** is all about. And it was generated by some experts in the field: fellow NHGC members. Their *Member Ideas* show you how to garden smartly, skillfully, sometimes even ingeniously.

In *"Planting Ideas—Seeds & Beyond"* you'll get member insights into propagating plants of all kinds successfully. No false or failed starts here–just growing results.

Then, in *"Space Savers & Good Lookers"* you'll find dozens of ideas for designing great gardens—even when space and time is tight. You don't have to be a professional landscape designer to create great gardens; sometimes a few great ideas are all you need to get started.

Of course, almost all of us utilize containers in our gardening, in one way or another. So we bring you *"Container Ideas by the Bushel."* See the creative ways that other members are container gardening ... then feel free to put the ideas to use around your home and patio.

Many of us experience the joys of wildlife in our gardens, but unfortunately our wild friends can sometimes bring heartache too, and they need to be removed in one way or another. *"All Critters Good & Bad"* gives tips and strategies for attracting the creatures you like, and ridding your garden of ones you don't quite appreciate.

Eating what we grow and harvest is a major pleasure for many gardeners. *"Healthy Plants, Happy Harvests"* offers up members' best ideas for making sure you get the results you want from your vegetables and herbs … and also presents some superb recipes for preparing your garden's bounty in the kitchen.

In *"Garden Solutions"* you'll find a wide variety of techniques for solving those garden challenges that are always cropping up. It would be nice to never have a gardening problem or quandary, but reality is that they just happen. Here are members' best ideas for solving them.

"The Rewards of Recycling" will take you to new heights of gardening efficiency—by using materials thoughtfully and skillfully, and being efficient with the soil and water resources you have. All these ideas will save you money as well, and who can complain about that? Of course, composting ideas are a part of this chapter too.

And lastly, we close with *"Bits 'n' Pieces"*—tidbits of gardening lore that otherwise don't neatly fit into one of the other categories, but nevertheless are real time- and worksavers you'll value.

We'll leave it to you to continue to find the time you need to garden. But when you are out there with your hands in the dirt and the sun shining down and a million tasks to do, turn toward some of the *Member Ideas* in this book and put your *Practical Gardening* skills to work.

Planting Ideas—
Seeds & Beyond

Nothing is quite as simple—or complex—as starting out your plants. Everything seems so simple, yet you want to be sure to do everything just right because there may only be one chance this year ...

Here are members' insights into successfully propagating plants of all kinds. Avoid false or failed starts—just get growing results.

Big Collards in Late-Season Fashion

Because I could never find collard plants in my area until late September, I tried planting seed in containers in June. By November I had my largest collards ever! I am so pleased with the results, I will continue doing this.

Virginia R. Price
Ashville, AL

Promoting the Layered Look

I like to propagate vines and shrubs by layering. It is easy to make babies of vines and shrubs such as honeysuckle, clematis, forsythia and dogwood, etc. At the end of summer, I select branches of vines that trail on the ground or bottom branches of shrubs as candidates for layering. I collect juice or milk cartons and remove the top and bottom to make an open cylinder. I pull the branches through these open containers so they can rest at a convenient spot on the branch (like a bracelet) and rest on the soil surface under the bush without stressing the branch. Then I tightly fill the carton from both ends with potting mix. I cover it with mulch and keep it moist. (Normal watering does it.)

I let it sit over winter. In spring, I sever the connection from the mother plant and continue watering for 2 weeks. As buds begin to open from the branch tips, I scoop up the transplants and transfer them to new spots or pots and fill with potting mix. These make excellent gifts or second plantings.

Rosy Chacko
Winslow, ME

No-Stoop Seed Planting

Cut the bottom off of a ½-gallon plastic milk jug. Tape about a 24-inch length of an old water hose to the spout of the milk jug. Then just walk down your garden rows and drop seed into your jug. You don't have to stoop over to plant seed. It sure saves the back!

Kathy Kinard
Livingston, TX

A Boxful of Seeds

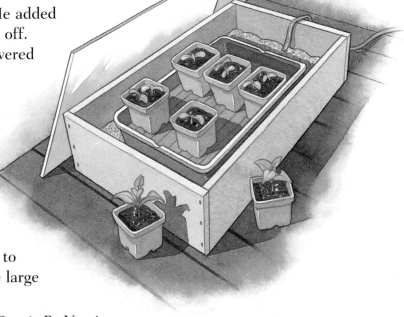

My husband built a 1-foot x 2-foot propagation box from scrap lumber. He added a clear plexiglass lid that can be lifted off. For a heating mat, we used a vinyl-covered waterbed heater that had its own thermostat. We placed the "heating mat" in the bottom of the box and covered it with a thin layer of builder's sand.

I start my seeds in 4-inch pots placed in a leakproof tray in the box so they can be watered from the bottom. When seedlings are about 1 inch tall, I move the pots to a sunny window. When the plants are large enough, I pot them up.

Dorris B. Norris
Saltillo, MS

Padding the Numbers

I have a trick for starting seeds that I have used for several years. Instead of buying those expensive seed-starting mats, I go to secondhand stores and buy old heating pads. I set my seeds in the starter trays, set the heating pads at the lowest setting and set the trays on them. I've always had great success using this method.

Dale Burgener
Bremerton, WA

Making a Stand Against Expense

I've always wanted one of those fancy light stands, but they're very expensive. Instead, I made my own. I started with a set of bookshelves that cost about $40 at a discount store. I chose a bookshelf that was white so it would reflect the light better. Then, in a short time, I put it together according to the instructions.

Next I bought six plant lights to attach to the shelves. Each plant light cost about $20, so my total cost was $160. That's still a lot of money, but it's much less than they charge for plant light stands in most catalogs and stores.

The bookshelf I made is 6 feet tall and 28 inches wide. The plant lights are 24 inches long. When you attach lights with screws, leave room at one end so you can plug in the cords.

This setup not only gives me plenty of light, but the shelves are adjustable, so you can move them up as the plants grow. Or you can set your plants on boxes, and just lower the plants as they grow. All of the lights are plugged in separately, so you can have as many turned on or off as you like. When I'm not growing plants, I use the bookshelf to store garden supplies.

Mitchell Lee Sunblade
Lincoln, NE

A Spicy Approach

To sow small seeds, use a spice jar or salt shaker and add a small amount of sand to the seeds. Then shake the mix into the garden or seed flats.

Shirley Wilcox
Nichols, NY

Editor's Tip

Germination and Growing Temperature for Various Vegetable and Herb Transplants

Crop	Germ. Temp (°F)	Days to Germ.	Growing Temp (°F)	Weeks to Transplant
Tomatoes	60–85	7–14	55–85	6–8
Eggplants	75–90	7–14	65–85	8–10
Peppers	65–95	7–14	65–85	8–10
Cabbage	45–95	4–12	55–75	4–6
Broccoli	45–85	4–12	55–75	4–6
Cauliflower	45–85	4–12	55–75	4–6
Brussels Sprouts	45–85	4–12	55–75	4–6
Lettuce	40–80	2–14	55–75	2–4
Basil	65–85	7–14	65–85	8–10
Parsley	50–85	14–28	55–75	10–12
Onions	50–95	7–14	55–75	6–8
Leeks	50–95	7–14	55–75	6–8
Celeriac	60–70	7–14	55–75	10–12

This chart lists the best temperature to start your seeds at, how long it takes for seeds to sprout when at these temperatures, and what temperatures are best for growing the plants. It's usually best to have warmer daytime temperatures than nighttime ones.

Seed-Starting Culture

If you don't have the space or the means for a seed mat, a yoghurt maker (often available for $2.00 at a garage sale) works very well to get those seeds up in a hurry. I put a handful of perlite in each compartment, then set a planted 2-inch flowerpot on top and put the yoghurt maker near a window. I don't need to cover it.

Irmgard Haskins
Garberville, CA

Eggs-Actly What Your Seeds Need

I used to have a hard time getting seedlings out of plastic starter kits at transplanting time. I have found that you can use the biodegradable bottoms from your cardboard egg cartons instead of the kits. Start your seeds in them as you would with plastic starter kits. Place a tray under them for drainage. The "egg-carton pots" can be planted right into the ground to avoid hurting the roots from transplant shock. (Always bury the carton section completely.)

Kimberly Tupper
International Falls, MN

Smiling Through Her Tiers

Cut tomato cages with wire cutters just above each tier. You will get 3 small rings for flowers, small shrubs or perennials. The mini-cages protect plants from dogs running over them, too. I also use them to mark where I planted seeds that will need support later.

Alma Olsen
River Rouge, MI

A Cagey Method

Cut tomato cages in half for use as a support for bushy plants such as peonies or mums. You can spray the cages green if you want them to blend with your garden.

Carole A. Woznicki
Itasca, IL

Tanks for the Tip

Here's my method of propagating African violets:

EQUIPMENT NEEDED:

1 10- or 20-gallon fish tank

1 light reflector to match the tank

**1 piece of glass or plastic ¼ inch thick to cover
the rest of the top of the tank**

1 pan, about 13 x 8 inches (1 inch or more deep)

Fill the pan with dampened vermiculite. Place it in the tank. Pour water into the tank to just below the depth of pan. Cut stems off African violets (about ¾-inch stem length to each leaf). Insert leaves into dampened vermiculite, about 1½ inches apart. Put the reflector and plate glass on top of the tank. Seal edges with clear plastic tape, or cover the top with plastic wrap and tape the edges down. Turn on the light. Leave it on at all times.

New plants will develop rapidly and will be ready to transplant in 3 to 5 weeks, depending on variety.

*Leslie J. Richardson
San Benito, TX*

Editor's Tip

Here's an easy, reusable plant support for pole beans, morning glories, moonflowers, and other seasonal climbers: Nail or staple chicken wire or hardware cloth to sturdy wooden poles. You can make multiple sections about 4 feet wide and add on as many as you need. When the harvest is over, just pull up the stakes and roll up your supports.

Swapping Ideas

I have a nifty trick for making packets for seed swapping. Cut your seed packets out of the bottom of junk-mail letters. Then tape one side, write seed and planting information on it, fill it with seed, and fold over and seal the top. You've got a quick, free seed packet ready to be wrapped in bubble paper or a padded mailer for swapping. Happy Gardening!

Kitty Elder
Liberty, NC

Herbs from a Pro

I have worked for an herb nursery as a greenhouse manager for the past 8 years and have come up with a very easy way to start new plants, especially herbs. Take a semi-soft cutting, about 2 inches, from any herb, such as thyme, sage, rosemary, savory, bay leaf, mint, lavender, lemon verbena or lemon balm. Strip away all the leaves, from the bottom up to about $1\frac{1}{2}$ inches from the top. Fill a pack (the little square pack holders that plants come in) with good potting soil. With your finger, make a hole and insert the cutting, cover with dirt and press lightly. Water well.

Keep the mix moist, but not soggy. You will have a new plant in about 6 weeks. When growth starts, nip out the top of the plant for bushier growth. Pop plants out of the plug compartments when you see the roots coming out of the bottom, and plant in a slightly bigger pot or plant in the ground. I do this at the nursery and don't need hormone powder.

Brenda Mason
Berkeley Springs, WV

Editor's Tip

To keep wooden stakes or trellises from rotting in the soil, use PVC piping as a planting hole. Cut about 8 to 12 inches of the proper width PVC—just large enough to fit the stake into. Pound the tube into the ground where the stake will go. Then place your stake or trellis leg in. Be sure not to let the tube fill with soil, or you'll have the same rot problem eventually. You can also use steel or aluminum piping the same way. Crimp the bottom for easier insertion into the ground.

From the Bottom Up

I use an old heating pad under plants that I am starting from seed. It warms the soil and you don't have to pay an expensive price for those gardening heating pads. Be sure to insert the heating pad in a heavy plastic sack to protect it from water.

John Butterworth
Via Email

Carry Out This Advice

Use Styrofoam containers in the garden in the spring when you plant seeds. Invert the container over the planted area—this will keep the moisture in (and critters out) until the seeds sprout.

Mary Anne McMurray
Monmouth Beach, NJ

Cake De-Icers

I take used clear plastic cake covers, drill ¼-inch holes in the side for ventilation, and put them over the cuke and melon seeds that I plant. This provides a mini-greenhouse to start the seeds faster and also protects them from critters. When the plants are pushing against the top of the covers, I remove them. I can start plants at least 2 to 3 weeks earlier with this method.

Lloyd Bahr
Camas, WA

Don't Toss 'em, Plant 'em

Instead of throwing cuttings from antique roses and artemisia into the compost, I often push the stems back into the ground as deep as they will go, leaving just a few leaves at the top. At least 50% of the time, they will grow into new plants to share with friends. This works especially well if the ground is wet from a rain. In the middle of our hot Texas summers, I put them in a shady, damp corner of the garden and transplant them to a sunny location when they're well established.

Pat Hayton
Grand Prairie, TX

Take Some Cuts

You can take root cuttings from impatiens and coleus easily in water. Break off all leaves that would be below the water. I use glass jars and place them out of the sun. When several roots emerge, pot up the plants and transplant them into beds or large pots in a few weeks.

Dorris Norris
Saltillo, MS

Pin Down the Tough Guys

Many seeds—moonflowers, morning glories and sweet peas, for example—have a hard shell on them. Spread them on wax paper or newspaper. Take a rolling pin and roll it lightly over the seeds. This will help break the hard seed coat. The seeds will have a much quicker start and you'll usually get a better stand of plants.

Elaine Mull
Jacksonville, FL

Gold Fingers

To get more goldenrod bushes, I cut a long limb from one already established and push it in the ground where I want it to grow permanently. I usually do this in the fall when it is moist most of the time. By using this method, I went from 6 bushes to almost 30.

Doris Jordan
Timberlake, NC

Editor's Tip

Yields of Fruits and Vegetables (25-foot rows)

Crop	Yield	Notes
Asparagus	8–10 lbs.	Over a 6 week harvest
Beans, Dry	25 lbs.	
Beans, Green	25 lbs.	For freezing and canning
Beans, Green	10 lbs.	Baby "filet" beans
Beets	25–35 lbs.	
Broccoli	25 lbs.	
Brussels Sprouts	5 lbs.	
Cabbage	40–50 lbs.	
Carrots	25 lbs.	For mature harvest
Carrots	15–20 lbs.	Baby carrots
Cauliflower	20–25 lbs.	
Celeriac	10–15 lbs.	
Celery	20–25 bchs.	
Cress	3–5 lbs.	
Cucumbers	25–35 lbs.	
Dandelion	3–5 lbs.	
Eggplant	20–25 lbs.	Less production in cool climates
Endive	20–25 lbs.	
Garlic	40–50 bulbs	
Kale	25–40 lbs.	Multiple harvests
Kohlrabi	15–20 lbs.	
Leeks	20–25 lbs.	
Lettuce	15–20 lbs.	If left to mature
Lettuce	3–5 lbs.	Cut for mesclun
Mâche	3–5 lbs.	
Mustard	25–40 lbs.	If left to mature
Mustard	3–5 lbs.	Cut for mesclun
Onions	25–40 lbs.	
Parsnips	25–30 lbs.	
Peas	8–10 lbs.	
Peppers	10–20 lbs.	Less production in cool climates
Potatoes	25 lbs.	
Pumpkins	50–75 lbs.	Depending on variety
Radishes	8–10 lbs.	
Shallots	15–20 lbs.	
Spinach	10–20 lbs.	Depending on size at harvest
Squash, Summer	5–25 lbs.	Depending on size at harvest
Squash, Winter	35–40 lbs.	Depending on variety
Sweet Corn	25–30 ears	Plant at least four rows in a block
Tomatoes	25–30 lbs.	
Turnips	15–25 lbs.	Depending on variety

These yields assume high fertility and plant density.

It Takes the Cake

The best seed-starter greenhouses I have found are the plastic sheet cake covers from supermarket bakeries. They are large (and a nice 4 ½ inches deep), readily available (free with your next birthday cake) and watertight.

Shirley J. Eklund
Chestertown, MD

Soaking Up Success

I soak hard seeds overnight in strong tea. The tannic acid softens the outer covering of the seeds and makes germination faster and surer.

Mary Ann Marino
West Pittsburgh, PA

Fencing in Veggies

I needed to put up a fence to keep my three large and very active dogs out of the garden. The fencing I used had wide spaces between the links. It is what some refer to as cow fencing, used by farmers as a fence line. I placed the fence on T-poles and tied it in place with old wire.

The cucumbers netted a bumper crop. I pickled 36 quarts and had enough left to use in salads and eat green. The squash netted dozens of full-sized ones. Cantaloupes also netted dozens of full-sized and medium fruits. The tomatoes and peppers had a bumper crop that I ate raw, froze, canned and gave away.

Steven Lee Wortman
Rhinelander, WI

Getting Crooks to Go Straight

To keep a shepherd's crook that holds birdfeeders or flower baskets straight, insert a $\frac{1}{2}$-inch galvanized or PVC pipe, about 18 inches long, into the ground. Sink it in straight until the top is about an inch or so below the surface. Slide the crook inside the pipe, and enjoy your nice straight display!

Norma Musser
Womelsdorf, PA

From the Ar-Chives

I love to plant chives throughout my garden every year. I let them bloom and flower because they attract ladybugs and butterflies, and I have never had any problems with "volunteer" chives. When the time comes to work up the garden in the fall, I rescue several chive plants and replant them in my flower beds, which are empty for the winter. Then, when spring comes I can remove the chives from the flower beds and divide them for the garden.

Sandra McKenzie
Braham, MN

An Easy Tie Holder

I use strips of pantyhose as plant ties. To keep them handier, I punch holes along the bottom edge of a cut plastic gallon jug and insert single knotted various lengths of nylon strips for easy access.

Vicki Broad
Hendersonville, NC

Cutting It Clothes

It seems that everyone in my household is very hard on clothing. Instead of throwing away old clothes such as T-shirts and khaki slacks, I cut them into long strips to use as ties in the garden. They're great for tying tomatoes to trellises, and do all the things I used to use twine for.

Aimee Ellis
Waveland, MS

Gathering Support

I love the natural look, not only to decorate a garden, but also to serve a useful purpose. So to support tall-growing flowers like yarrow, Oriental lilies and loosestrife, I make fences from twigs and small branches of trees. They are easily found in the woods after a wind or rainstorm. I cut these twigs and branches in the right size to form a fence. I hold them together with nails and then wrap pieces of bark around the "joints" and tie or nail them in place. Then I push or pound the fence into the ground.

I have had some of these fences for years. They seem to look better with age, hold up extremely well over the years and look natural and decorative in the gardens.

Mary Ann Marino
West Pittsburgh, PA

Editor's Tip

When setting up a trellis against a wall or fence, leave "breathing room" for the trellis and the plants it supports. Use 1- or 2-inch spacers between the wall and the trellis. This prevents the wall, fence or trellis from rotting because of trapped moisture, and also provides air flow around the climbing plant. You can use old thread spools, dowels, or cut-up pieces of PVC pipe as spacers. Creating breathing room with spacers is also a good idea for window boxes.

From Benches to Beach Boulders

I had some old bench presses that I covered with ½-inch wire mesh. Then I cemented over the forms to make "boulders". I even added a local flair because I live near the beach—I attached seashells with cement.

Gene Requa
Del Mar, CA

Best Roses, Bar None

I use a ½-inch rebar 20 feet long for my climbing roses. I stick one end into the ground and then arch it to the desired width. Then I attach the roses by wrapping the canes around the rebar. This causes the roses to cascade when they bloom.

John Butterworth
Via Email

Seeds in a Tube

Instead of purchasing peat pots to start seeds, cut toilet paper tubes in half, and set them in a plastic tray. Fill with potting soil and plant seeds.

Diana Smith
Kelso, WA

Picture-Perfect Labels

Laminate empty seed packets or cut out pictures of plants from seed catalogs. Put them in the tines of plastic forks and place the handle in the soil where your seeds or plants are. These labels are weatherproof and can be reused.

Darlene Reinoehl
Klingerstown, PA

Light That Bends

I use fluorescent shop lights to grow my seedlings and have discovered that metal coat hangers make the best holders for the lights. I start with six hangers on each light and move them when necessary as the seedlings grow. The coat hangers are easy to adjust simply by bending them, and because of this the lights always hang evenly.

Sandra McKenzie
Braham, MN

Build
An Arbor

Here's how to build an arched
or square arbor. The widely
spaced braces allow room for
robust plants to climb, but are far
enough apart to discourage small
children from using the arbor as
a jungle gym. Lattice can be cut
to size and attached to the arbor
with locking plastic ties.

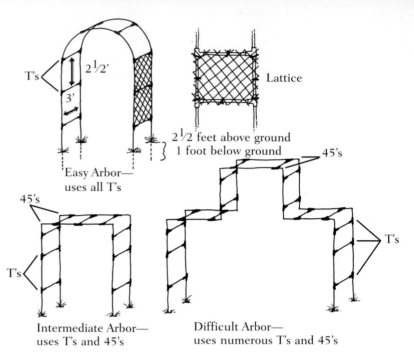

T's 2½' 3'

Lattice

2½ feet above ground
1 foot below ground

Easy Arbor—
uses all T's

45's

45's

T's

T's

Intermediate Arbor—
uses T's and 45's

Difficult Arbor—
uses numerous T's and 45's

MATERIALS NEEDED:

PVC ½-inch tubing, 10
feet or longer, about 8 or 9

PVC ½-inch T's, about 14

PVC cement

Plastic lock ties

**LATTICE
MATERIALS NEEDED:**

PVC tubing

PVC T's for arched top

PVC 45's for square top

Lattice

Plastic lock ties

*Linda Garbow
Middleville, MI*

Support Hose

Many of our flowers are heavy so we
support the plants with cut-up nylon
pantyhose tied to wooden posts around
the plants. The nylon stretches as
needed and doesn't hurt plant stems.

*Taisija Aunins
Elkhart, IN*

A Stake for Your Back

Take a hollow bamboo stake about 36 inches long, and cut a slant off the bottom. Then drop seed through the stake into garden rows. For smaller seeds, add sand and slide seeds down the tube to the garden. This sure saves the back.

Shirley Wilcox
Nichols, NY

Tearing Through the Tasks

Old T-shirts make good plant ties. If there aren't any side seams, just make one cut from the bottom (at the width you want the ties to be) and start tearing. The strip will go around and around the shirt in a continuous strip to be cut into whatever lengths you want.

Betty J. Burke
Odessa, TX

Editor's Tip

When tying up tomato vines or other plants, do it correctly so the tender green parts don't get rubbed or squeezed. Use a figure-eight pattern by making one loop for the plant and another for the stake.

A Bunch of Swingers

We had a large swing-slide-climbing bar set for toddlers up to 80 pounds. When our two kids grew into teenagers we were faced with taking down the swing set, but the bars were held in the ground with cement blocks and very heavy to dig up and dispose of.

My husband had the idea to leave the bars and spray paint them forest green. He drilled holes for the chair swing we ordered from a catalog. I planted white potato vines on either side supported by a wooden trellis. We placed down river rock to border the sitting area. This spring the vines met in the middle and cascaded over the top. They have prolific white flowers nearly year-round in our mild East Bay climate. It's a wonderful spot to sit in the morning and enjoy the garden.

Helen Botsford
Antioch, CA

Savvy Supports

I like to use tomato supports for tall bulbs like glads, freesia and acidanthera. They also work great to raise asparagus ferns.

Pam Ellis
Phoenix, AZ

Grapes in Bunches

Here's my easy, simple method for propagating grapes. Do this from late December to mid-January:

1. Make 20-inch-long cuttings of pencil-thick, brown, woody grape vines. Make sure you line each cut in the direction the grape vine grew. This will be the top of each cutting.

2. Insert the bottom of each cutting into a container of moist sphagnum peat moss. I usually place about a half-dozen cuttings in one larger container. The container must have drainage holes. Insert the cutting 10 inches deep.

3. Set the container outdoors for the entire winter. Let snow or rain water it.

4. In spring, buds on the stems will start to swell, eventually forming leaves.

5. Allow 6 to 8 weeks of growth for proper root development.

6. Upend the container (do not pull out plants) and pot up individually to give to friends, or plant in the yard. It takes 3 years of growth for vines to bear fruit.

Edwin T. Kapustka
Des Plaines, IL

Flat-Picking Champ

When planting small seeds in pots, wet the wide end of a flat toothpick and touch the seeds. The toothpick picks up one seed at a time, eliminating wasted seed.

Lee Grillo
Jackson, MS

Space Savers &
Good Lookers

What to plant where, and how to make it all

look great, are age-old gardening challenges.

Sometimes a few ideas are all you need.

Here are dozens of ideas for designing great

gardens—even when space and time is tight.

Make the most of every inch of your gardening

space.

A Colorful Block Party

Instead of planting marigolds with cinder-block borders, I thought it would be better to plant them inside the holes in the blocks. After filling each individual hole with soil, I planted my "Dwarf Mix Marigolds" in their new homes. Now, not only are the plants a natural insect deterrent, they also add a wonderful array of color to the many greens growing nearby.

Renee M. Caillouet
Gary, LA

R.F.D. Gardenland

Place a rural-type mailbox (the kind with two doors and a slot for newspapers and magazines) on a post near your garden. Keep your hand tools, labels, gloves and twine there and you'll save many a step. Be sure to include some plastic bags for impromptu harvest of cucumbers, beans, peas, peppers, tomatoes, broccoli, and so forth.

Mitzi Earl
Salem, AR

Overlapping Uses

Do not discard the blades (plastic or metal) of old venetian blinds. Cut the 1-inch blades about 8, 10 or 12 inches long and use them as name labels for plants. The wider ones can be split in half. If you use permanent ink, they will last a long time.

Kurken V. Kirk
Kingston, NY

A Shining Example

This is a lighthouse my husband, Ed, built to cover up a well head in our front yard. Then he installed a 100-gallon pond surrounded by Pennsylvania ledge stone. We made little beds between the stones and planted purple and white alyssum along with assorted grasses. Ed also made the mooring post wrapped in rope. We stocked the pond with goldfish and installed a pond heater to keep them alive through the winter. The small footbridge will connect with another smaller pond. We made an unsightly area of our yard into a small oasis. We love it!

Sherry Winters
Olivet, MI

A Picture-Perfect Look

Chrysanthemums do not all make it through the winter, so I take a picture when they are blooming. In the spring, I can look at the picture and know which ones need replacing before I move them back outside. Also, I can see how to arrange the colors so all the yellows or reds are not in one spot.

Carole Kopietz
Norfolk, NE

Mower to the Point

Design the shape of garden beds and borders with your lawn mower. Just mow areas that will become the perimeter of your beds. This will save lots of mowing time later by avoiding odd-angled corners, too-sharp turns, and cramped areas.

Mrs. Teri Caddle
Clayton, IL

Glad to Help

In spring, when bulbs are blooming, if I notice an area that needs bulbs for next year, I plant gladiolus bulbs in it. Then in the fall, when I dig the gladiolus, I plant the new spring bulbs, and kill two birds with one stone. This has really helped me to balance my beds and get things placed just the way I want them.

Brenda Shearer
Bourbon, IN

Gardening for the Winter

When creating planting areas, try to consider all four seasons and the view from inside the house, especially in the winter. For example, ornamental grasses are lovely in the snow; redtwig and yellowtwig dogwoods brighten up the winter scene; and plants with winter berries are appreciated by the birds.

I don't cut back all my perennials in the fall. I especially like to leave black-eyed Susans and purple coneflowers for winter interest (and bird food, too).

Shirley Polen
Durand, MI

A Boulder Approach

For years we had huge rocks in our yard that couldn't be moved. We had to mow and trim in and around them until I decided to connect them with other large rocks I brought in. I filled the area with soil from our veggie garden, and it made a wonderful flower bed.

Janet Park
Oakland, MD

A Storehouse on Wheels

Use your car trunk to store stuff (birdseed, potting soil, sand, winter de-icers) that is too heavy to put anywhere else. The trunk gives me a handy level to work from, and critters don't get into things like birdseed. The extra weight also helps traction.

Sue Tummonds
State College, PA

Paperless Planning

I know of an easy way for "computer gardeners" to keep a garden journal/calendar. If your computer runs Windows programs, create a new notepad document. Open it, and type .LOG. Whenever you open it, it will automatically put the date on it. I keep this on my computer desktop, and it makes it really simple to keep track of when plants start to bloom, when I fertilize, etc. In the winter, I use it to plan what I need to move, and it's really helpful for making plant combinations. Also, it means less paper for me to shuffle on the desk!

Brenda Shearer
Bourbon, IN

Editor's Tip

Invasive perennials—such as lily-of-the-valley, mints and bamboo—can spread throughout your garden if you grow them as you would other plants. To avoid this, grow invasives in containers. These plants look good in pots or boxes, and in the case of the mints, you can bring them in over the winter. If you have a sunny window, you can harvest the leaves year-round. (Be sure to cut the flower heads off before they go to seed.) For a permanent contained bed, cut the bottom out of the container. The plant can set its roots down more deeply. But check periodically for escapees!

It's in the Bag

My hint may be helpful to people with physical disabilities, poor soil or not enough time to till the ground.

Simply buy bags of premixed potting soil. Line up the unopened bags to make your flower beds. Punch a few holes in the bottom for drainage and plant directly into the bags. Apply mulch or decorative gravel to cover the bags around the plants. This works great! Also, the next planting season, you can remove the mulch and open the bags. After adding plant food and scattering the soil, you're ready to go again! Using the bags all but ends the need for weeding.

Karen Daniel
Atlanta, TX

Editor's Tip

If neighbor kids or large animals enter your yard too often, try a "friendly fence." Plant thorny raspberry or blackberry plants thickly enough to form a hedge. In a year you'll have a thorny barrier that will keep out unwelcome visitors, yet look good and provide you with lots of fruit. Roses are good for this too, especially vigorous, gnarly ones such as the sweetbriar or Eglantine (*Rosa eglanteria*), which can live for decades.

Wired to the Task

I love to make cucumber pickles—dill, sweets, sliced, all kinds—but my garden is small and cucumbers take space. So I plant my seeds in a solid row. I thin seedlings to about 6 inches apart and then drive stakes about 10 inches from the row on both sides. Then I tack chicken wire on the stakes. The cucumbers stay within the frame and are easy to pick.

Mrs. Stanley Dalton
Mountain Grove, MO

An Edible Groundcover

My yard is fenced with chain-link fencing. When I took a good look at my lot, I found that I had 12 inches of space between the edge of the curb and the fence space. This space required a lot of upkeep to remain tidy until I decided to utilize the space and cut down on maintenance.

I filled the space with good topsoil and planted everbearing strawberries there. Not only have they served as a nice décor, but they have produced a bountiful crop each of the past two years. I simply watch for runners and insert the new runner, and voilà—a new plant and more berries!

Everyone said passersby would harvest my crop, but they haven't. People just stop and admire my space-saver bed and chuckle at the idea of strawberries at curbside.

Lillian Harms
Milwaukie, OR

Arch Angles

I made the arch over the white bench at the back of my garden out of PVC pipe (available from any plumbing supply store). First, take 2-foot lengths of metal pipe and hammer them halfway into the ground. The PVC pipe fits right over the pipe. With this arch, there's no painting, no rotting and no falling trellises. Morning glories, hyacinth bean vine or any quick-growing annual vine looks great on it.

Elaine Watson
Louisville, KY

Controlling Cukes

Use this technique to save space and time when growing cucumbers: Take a full hog-wire panel and bend it to the desired height. (I make mine just high enough to walk under.) Hold each end down with a steel T-post. I use a piece of bailing wire to hold it in place. Then I bank my soil along the bottom.

When the cucumbers start to send out tendrils, train the vine up the panel. You need to be persistent when doing this, or the vine will go everywhere. Your cucumbers will be easy to pick this way.

Russell Harvey
Leighton, IA

Buckets of Bounty

You can grow tomatoes without using cages around them. Just take a 5-gallon bucket with a handle and put five holes in the bottom big enough for small tomato plants. Then, turn it right side up and fill it with soil. Put a lid over it and turn it upside down again. Plant your tomatoes in the holes. Let it sit for a day or two, then turn it right side up and hang it by the handle. Your plants will grow toward the ground. I take some of the soil out of the top when I hang it up so it's easier to water.

Also, because they are above ground, you don't get a lot of the bugs bothering your plants. Big tomatoes do just fine; the branches get stronger as they get heavier. To water the bucket, I just pour a gallon or so of water in the top. The extra water drains out the bottom holes that the tomatoes grow through.

People are amazed at how tomatoes grow this way. It lets people who don't have much space still grow tomatoes.

Carole Wilmoth
Bandera, TX

Editor's Tip

When laying out either raised beds or regular ground-level planting areas, be sure you leave beds only wide enough to reach into from either side—generally about 4 feet. Otherwise you may have to step into the bed and risk compacting the soil.

Space Saver

BEFORE

AFTER

My husband and I live in a typical Chicago bungalow. There is not a big garden area in the backyard for vegetables or herbs—just an 18-foot, 30-inch-wide strip along the south side of the garage.

To utilize this space to the maximum, I screwed in wooden slats along the top and bottom of the garage wall and added galvanized roofing nails 3 inches apart along the slats. Then I strung electrical wire top to bottom around each nail. The height of each wire is 78 inches. I only need 3 inches against the garage wall to plant my seeds, and the rest of the earth is free for my non-climbing plants. The cost of this "wall garden" was about $25.

Nancy Garcia
Chicago, IL

A Ton from a Tunnel

The "green tunnel" (pictured below) was the solution to my tight space and short growing season. It's made out of cattle panels, which are precut 4-foot x 16-foot fence panels available from farm supply stores and building centers. They cost approximately $12 each. To construct your own "green tunnel," drive stakes into the ground in two rows approximately 8 feet apart. Bow the panels to fit in between the stakes, and use a couple of pieces of scrap wire to tie each panel to the next one. Make the tunnel as long as you want by adding panels.

The tunnel shown in the photograph consists of 4 panels (16 feet long.) This past year, it supported 2 cucumber vines, 2 birdhouse gourd vines, 12 tomato vines, and 16 pole-bean vines. Cucumbers, tomatoes and beans were a pleasure to pick from inside and outside of the tunnel. The shade helped to keep moisture in the ground and provided an ideal environment for growing lettuce and spinach that I planted in rotation, even throughout the hottest part of the summer.

Daniel Sargent
Hutchinson, MN

From Has-Been to Nice Bin

To construct a quick and inexpensive compost bin, just go to a recycling company or a trucking warehouse and get four wooden shipping pallets. (Many places will give them away.) Then nail or wire the edges together sturdily in a box shape, and you'll have a neat bin. Fasten one edge so you can open it, to stir or remove compost. This bin is very easy to breakdown and store in winter and reassemble in spring. If slatted sides are too wide, just run some screen or plastic netting around the sides.

Shirley Wilcox
Nichols, NY

 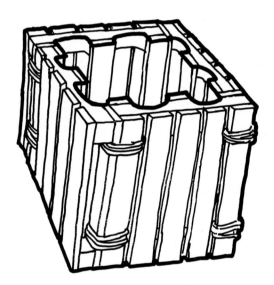

A Mini "Kitchen Garden"

To show the measurements and shape accurately when planning to make a garden bed, use a tablecloth as your basic plot. Use a variety of circular, oblong, and square objects such as coasters, glasses, plates and knick-knacks to represent beds, containers, plants, hedges, ponds and the like.

Judith Youngblood
Great Neck, NY

North

Dappled
Shade
1

Open
Shade
2

Medium
Shade
3

Deep
Shade
4

Making Light of the Situation

To get an idea where I could best grow my plants, I watched where the sun went in my yard every 2 or 3 hours. I sketched a picture of the sun/shade ratio. As it turned out, there was only one spot that would get enough sun for vegetables and herbs. Most of the garden was partially shaded at different times of the day, which is all right for many perennials. I found good reason to move some things that didn't get enough sun or enough shade, so my "sun-spotting" really paid off.

Elaine Watson
Louisville, KY

Working the Angles

Here's an easy measuring device: Cut a cardboard triangle with sides the length of the spacing you want for your plants. For example, if you're planting at 6-inch intervals, make each side 6 inches long. Use the triangle to set plants or seeds at exact spacing, or use the triangle to find the distance between rows, then stagger the seeds every other row.

Carol Frederick
Ambridge, PA

Editor's Tip

If you're stuck with a serviceable—but ugly—chain-link fence, dress it up with some enamel paint. Black and dark green are good choices because they blend into the landscape visually. A rule of thumb: A 4-foot-high chain-link fence will take about a quart of paint per 20 feet of length.

Container Ideas
by the Bushel

Whether you live in a city townhome or
apartment, a home in town or in a suburb, or
on several acres of land in the country,
containers almost certainly take some role in
your gardening plan.

Here are creative ways that other members
are container gardening: Ideas they want you
to borrow (even call your own!), and put to
good use.

A Nice Gift, to Boot

I planted flowers in a 2-liter bottle, and filled the toe of a pair of old high-buckle boots (that our dad used to wear) with rocks. Then I put the bottle into the "leg" of the boots, making a bunch of boot planters for Father's Day and also sharing them with the family.

Colleen Gates
Monee, IL

A Panel Solves Orchid Problems

I have been growing orchids under home conditions, using fluorescent lights. They require 50% humidity with plants set on gravel in trays containing water. However, this caused an algaecide sludge buildup. I eliminated this condition by purchasing (at a building supply store) 2-foot x 4-foot plastic ceiling light panels. I placed two panels, one on top of the other, in $1\frac{1}{2}$-inch-deep trays. Plants are out of water and resting level on the plastic panels, but still enjoying the extra humidity.

Walter Burdett
Lyons, IL

A Concrete Idea

A plastic birdbath can be the mold for an expensive-looking plant stand. Just fill it with concrete. After it dries, cut the plastic off.

Diana Smith
Kelso, WA

Pining for a Handier Container

You can use pinecones in the bottom of larger planters to make the containers lighter and easier to move. They add organic matter to the soil mix, too.

Susan Holster
Newton, AL

Sweet Success

To start my own sweet potato plants about 10 weeks before the last frost, I take a 1-gallon plastic jug and cut the top off. Then, depending on how many plants I want, I take one or two small (3-inch-diameter by 3-inch-high) plastic containers and wire them to the gallon jug at the top. I then cut one or two small holes in them to hold the sweet potato from falling through so that it is sticking up and down in the water also. As the sprouts grow, I put chicken wire around them to keep them from falling over. I fill the jug with water halfway up the sweet potatoes. About 10 days before the last frost, I break off the sprouts and stick them in 3 inches of water or until they get roots. Then I plant them about 12 inches apart in hills about 5 inches or 6 inches above the normal level of the ground. (Sweet potatoes don't like it too wet.) I mulch them also. Works every time!

Clayton Pflug
Beaver Falls, PA

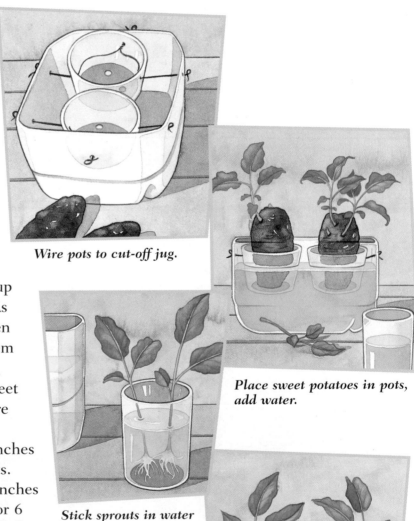

Wire pots to cut-off jug.

Place sweet potatoes in pots, add water.

Stick sprouts in water to root.

Plant sprouts in ground.

A Mulch That Really Rocks

Place stones, such as smooth river rock, on top of soil in planter pots or even houseplant pots. This serves two purposes: It can help retain soil moisture and keep rain from splashing out the dirt, and in houseplants it will keep cats from scratching in the soil. It also looks attractive.

Darlene Reinoehl
Klingerstown, PA

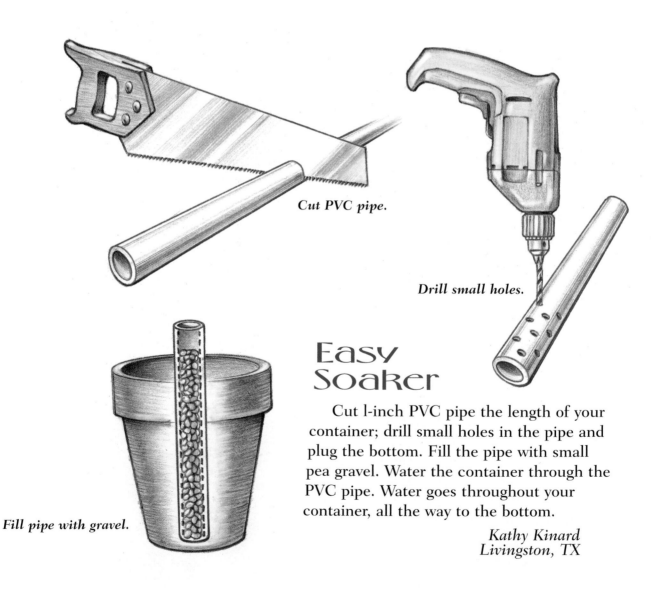

Cut PVC pipe.

Drill small holes.

Fill pipe with gravel.

Easy Soaker

Cut l-inch PVC pipe the length of your container; drill small holes in the pipe and plug the bottom. Fill the pipe with small pea gravel. Water the container through the PVC pipe. Water goes throughout your container, all the way to the bottom.

Kathy Kinard
Livingston, TX

A "Grate" Recycled Container

I saved this fireplace insert from a neighbor's barnyard. Chickens had found it a nice roost, so it took quite a while to clean, but it was worth it.

After moving it to the front of my rock garden, I lined the inside with heavy plastic, put in potting soil, and planted a variety of annuals and ivy.

Cheryl McAtee
Vancouver, WA

Good News by Mail

Plantings around my mailbox have always been a problem. Too much road salt, road debris and rocks made the ground a terrible place to plant. It was also a difficult spot to mow and took a lot of time with the hand trimmers. I had great results this year, however, by planting my annual flowers in large pots (plastic or clay), digging holes to the depth of the pots, and dropping them into the depressions.

Sinking the pots saved on extra watering, and when it came time to mow and trim around the mailbox, I just lifted the pots, set them aside, mowed down the grass and returned the pots to their respective places. The flowers bloomed beautifully and it really saved wear and tear on my back and hands. I didn't fill in the holes this fall and I cleaned and saved the same pots to be reused next year.

L. Decker
Clymer, PA

Editor's Tip

When frost threatens tomatoes or other tender plants, here's a quick fix: Surround the plant with an old tire. Add warm water to the inside of the tire. Stack tires if necessary and cover the plant with cardboard or plastic. Remove the cover when frost has passed. This keeps the air and soil warmer around tender plants. It's also an inexpensive way to get a jump on the season in cold areas.

Box 'em Up

If you would like to grow a garden but don't have, or need, a large area, try this: Use old-fashioned flower boxes. To gain additional growing space, I place them in my garden and along the edges of the ramp into the home. They adapt to any vegetable. I have grown the following in boxes: tomatoes, peppers, cucumbers, squash, cantaloupe, watermelon, radishes, beets and carrots.

I personally find the best size to be a 1-foot x 1-foot x 3-foot box. Because this is a homemade flower box, it can be made out of scrap wood and painted.

Steven Lee Wortman
Rhinelander, WI

A Prescription for a Healthy Tree

One of my biggest indoor trees sits on a carpet so I recycled an old bath container from a hospital visit to hold the tree and its pot. It's just the right size and no runoff water goes onto the carpet. I haven't yet found a container with a dish that will hold all the runoff water and the only other thing to do is to water the plant too little or water it several times, which is not an option for a busy person or a healthy plant.

Rachelle Maltzman
Brooklyn, NY

An Open-and-Shut Idea

I use a small pinecone to determine when my houseplants need to be watered. It closes up when the soil is wet and opens when it dries out. Looks interesting too!

Elizabeth Seibert
Katonah, NY

A Tub for Thugs

I purchased a primrose (*Oenothera*) several years ago. After one season it was taking over my flower bed. I fought this aggressive plant for a couple of seasons before I found a solution. (I absolutely love the bloom of this plant, otherwise I probably would have dug it up.) Instead, I purchased a large plastic tub, made drainage holes in the bottom, and filled it with potting soil. I dug up the primrose plant, divided it and discarded some. The remainder of the plant I transplanted to the soil-filled tub. To my delight, this idea (so far) has kept the aggressor in check.

Kathryn Palmer
Canton, IL

Planting a Bag of Peanuts

When filling large planters, use the Styrofoam peanut-shaped pellets for drainage. They are lightweight. Placing them in a mesh (such as an onion sack) will make cleanup easier when you have to redo the planter.

Mitzi Earl
Salem, AR

Hang Out with Pop

I cut and paint 2-liter pop bottles and use them as hanging baskets. They are inexpensive and can be hung anywhere.

Karen Schielke
Muldrow, OK

Editor's Tip

If you have large containers sitting outside on a hard surface, place round pebbles or gravel under them. The small rocks act as ball bearings whenever you need to scoot a pot around a little or rotate it. The rocks also act as a drainage aid, by letting excess water flow away.

Free Containers

My garden tip consists of recycling at least two materials—5-gallon plastic buckets and aluminum cans—that are filling our disposal sites quite needlessly.

MATERIALS:

1. **One 5-gallon plastic bucket, which can be obtained free from a fish market, deli, etc.**

2. **Several aluminum cans that have been emptied and rinsed.**

Clean and rinse out the bucket if needed. Either drill or punch out about eight holes (no larger than $\frac{1}{2}$ inch; dirt may run out otherwise) around the base of the bucket. Do not punch holes in the very bottom. This will weaken the base of the bucket.

The cans can be placed in the bottom to make the bucket lighter in case you have to move it. Otherwise, the cans could be omitted and the bucket could be entirely filled with soil mix. However, when the bucket is filled with soil only, it's quite heavy to move.

Fred Erickson
West Babylon, NY

A Microclimate for Top Tomatoes

Every year I grow tomato plants in large containers in order to better control the amount of heat and direct sunlight they get. I set the containers on my back steps next to the house, where they get plenty of southwest exposure. Heat radiating off the house provides a nice warm environment for them. I make sure I water often so they don't dry out with the additional heat they are getting. Growing them in containers close to the back entrance also allows me to bring the plants into the porch to protect them from early or late frosts. I can also pick them easily.

Tami Anderson-Olsen
Calumet, MI

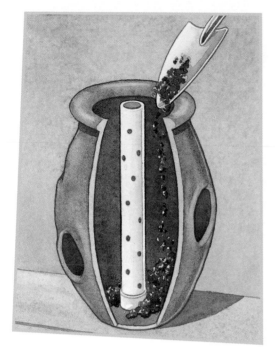

Cut pipe, drill holes, place pipe in jar, add soil.

Water plant through the pipe.

For the Berries

I always found it difficult to water strawberry jars until I came up with this idea. My husband cut a piece of PVC pipe the depth of the pot, capped the bottom, and drilled holes at different intervals up and down the pipe. When planting, place the pipe in the center while filling the jar with plants and soil. Then pour water into the top of the pipe to water all the plants.

Norma Musser
Womelsdorf, PA

A Hot Tip for Drainage Holes

If you have a plastic container you want to use as a planter, don't try to punch drainage holes. Instead, burn the holes into the planter using the heated point of an old Phillips-head screwdriver. I use deep plastic drainage saucers for mini-cactus and succulent gardens, and by burning the drain holes, the containers don't crack. Shallow mixing bowls also make good pots for succulents, cacti and snake plants.

Betty Burke
Odessa, TX

No More Tired Old Planters!

For container gardening, paint automobile tires with bright paints to add color and interest to the garden. My local tire store was more than happy to give me their old tires and I painted them with Premium accent Colors by Valspar, interior/exterior latex gloss enamel. This paint is effective

because it contains crystalline silica which adheres to the tires better than pure latex paint. Additionally, thick tires work best because they are stiffer than thin tires and thus the paint is less likely to crack and chip off when the tires are handled.

Painting these tires is so much fun and the result is bound to get comments from garden visitors. Fill the bottom of the tire walls with a layer of rocks to provide drainage, then fill the rest of the way up with a mixture of one-third topsoil, one-third compost, and one-third peat moss.

Christine Simmons
Seattle, WA

Critters, No; Drainage, Yes

I place pieces of hardware cloth over the drainage holes of all my containers. My recommendation is the $^{1}/_{4}$-inch or $^{1}/_{2}$-inch mesh size of hardware cloth: Window screening is too small in size and results in clogging.

Bonsai growers have used this method to maximize usable soil space. Hardware cloth prevents slugs, snails and others from entering soil from the bottom. Plus, it increases drainage, which is so important.

Philip Greig
Walnut Creek, CA

No Mis-Stake Plant Supports

When you have to move and are worried about your taller houseplants, try "staking" them with inexpensive bamboo chopsticks, fondue sticks or skewers. They are the perfect size for most houseplants that need a little temporary support. They eventually decay, but they are perfect for support for up to 3 to 5 months. I used them for moving tall cacti that tend to tip over in the pot and for temporary support after repotting.

Jill McMahan
Indianapolis, IN

Editor's Tip

The right kind of container may help a plant survive. Remember, clay (terra-cotta) pots are more porous, so they are less likely than plastic to retain too much water. But they may need more frequent watering in hot times. Correspondingly, plastic retains water better, but plants in plastic may need less frequent watering to avoid root-rot problems.

Chapter Four

All Critters Good & Bad

Wildlife can bring great joy, and sometimes great heartache, to the garden. Birds, butterflies, insects, animals—sometimes you love them, sometimes you don't.

Here are tips and strategies for attracting the creatures you like, and ridding your garden of ones you don't quite appreciate.

Uncanny Cutworms

Here is my garden tip to protect tomato and pepper plants from cutworms. I find an 8-oz. tomato sauce can (2½ inches in diameter and 3 inches high is ideal). I cut the top and bottom out of the can. Then I place the can 1½ inches deep in the soil—this leaves 1½ inches above ground. At the end of the growing season you just throw the can away and start saving cans for the next year's growing season.

Bernard Johnson
Honeoye Falls, NY

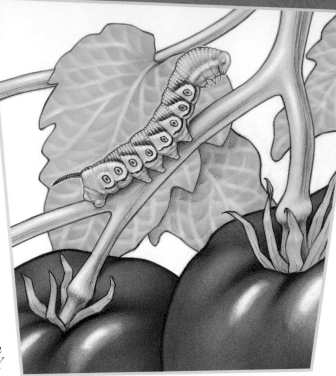

Slipping One Over on the Squirrels

Many people come across problems with squirrels getting into their birdfeeders. Here's an easy solution. Take one of those iron hangers you buy for hanging baskets and sink it into your lawn away from your trees. Hang a birdfeeder on one arm and a hanging basket, hummingbird feeder or lawn ornament on the other side. Then, use cooking oil or Crisco to grease the stem of the hanger. It's safe for the squirrels and is very amusing to watch them slide!

Kellie Senerchia
Hawley, PA

Stuffing Himself in the Garden

I found out that the old-fashioned idea of setting a scarecrow sitting in a chair near my vegetable garden really worked! It kept the native whitetail deer away and out of my garden. Plus, the scarecrows are fun to make. My 10-year-old nephew and I had fun putting him together.

Laura Morrow
Newton, NJ

Gone in a Flash

The Mylar wine containers (boxed wine dispensers) and free CD-ROMs that get mailed to you are great for keeping birds away from your plants. The Mylar bags can be cut in strips and hung under patios or in your garden. Mylar and the disks both flash brightly in the sun, and move easily with slight breezes. Hang them wherever birds and creatures eat your grapes and other fruits.

Rosemary DePumpo
Waverly, NY

It's Too Darned Hot...

Inexpensive bulk cayenne pepper (powder form) from discount stores is a great pest deterrent. I sprinkle it everywhere and often. It saves my bulbs and hostas from squirrels and rabbits.

Rosemary DePumpo
Waverly, NY

Editor's Tip

If you like to attract lots of birds and have some extra space, make a high-volume, informal sunflower patch in the spring. Buy a bag of bird-feed sunflower seeds and scatter the seed over the area. Cover the seeds with a little soil and water them down. Thin as needed and let the seedheads mature for the birds to eat. Not all the seeds will come up, but this will be quicker and less expensive than planting a more formal sunflower patch in garden style.

A Real Bird Dog

I didn't have a single squirrel at my birdfeeder this winter. I discovered that my dog enjoys spending time outdoors watching the birds, so I tie him out by the feeder for a little while every day. The birds don't mind his company. Apparently, the doggie scent around the feeder keeps the squirrels at bay even when "Keeper" is indoors taking his afternoon nap.

Cheryl McAtee
Vancouver, WA

Rock-Solid Protection

To keep squirrels, chipmunks or cats from digging in your containers, place 1- to 2-inch stones in the soil in the pot. The stones are large enough to frustrate the critters and they serve as a mulch too.

Rose Anne Wheeler
Willingboro, NJ

Tearing into the Task

Every year when I set out plants (peppers, tomatoes, any new young plant) in my garden, I tear newspaper into 3- by 9-inch strips and wrap them around the young plants where they go into the soil. This keeps cutworms from biting stems off.

Also, as the pepper plants begin to grow, I take small tree branches that have fallen and stick them in the soil around my plants to keep the birds from picking the tops off until the plants get strong. I do this with 100% success.

Rose Boyer
Hecker, IL

Beetles Rue the Day...

We've had Japanese beetles destroying our rose bushes. Last year we experimented with the herb rue (*Ruta graveolens*), and planted four rue plants around our rose bush. It worked! I believe it is the scent that keeps the little pests away. It is also a natural alternative to insecticides, which my fiancé and I tend to stay away from. (Note: Some people get dermatitis from handling rue—be careful when touching the leaves.)

Kellie Senerchia
Hawley, PA

Editor's Tip

To attract more kinds of birds, set feeders out at different heights and areas of the yard. Keep just one kind of seed in each feeder; don't mix seeds if you want to minimize squabbling. Smaller birds can find their own feeder without fighting with bigger birds or predators.

Wrap Up Your Problems

My gardening tip is for protection against cutworms (my folks always did this and I always have too—and I'm 77 now). First, take a piece of newspaper and make some little strips about 3 to 4 inches long and about 2 inches wide. Then wrap them around your peppers, tomatoes, cabbages or any other plants. Keep about an inch above the ground and the rest in the ground. I do this with all early plants I set out. I've never lost any plants from cutworms this way.

Rosa Putnam
Vassar, MI

Sticking It to Cutworms

Many people are bothered with cutworms cutting their plants—particularly tomatoes. The solution is so simple you might find it hard to believe. Get a stick about 6 inches long and stick it down beside your plant (about $\frac{1}{8}$ inch from the plant). With the stick there the cutworm can't wrap around your plant. If it can't wrap around the plant it can't cut it.

James Bricker
Leesville, LA

Recipe for Bug Traps

Take a 1-gallon plastic milk jug with the cap on. Cut a half-dollar-size hole on the side opposite from the handle and up toward the top a bit. Into this hole drop 2 banana skins, 2 cups vinegar (I use apple cider vinegar), 1 cup sugar, and $\frac{1}{2}$ to 1 cup molasses, and fill it up with warm water until half of the jug is filled. Stir or shake until all contents are mixed, and hang 2 or 3 per tree. I have an apple, a pear and 3 cherry trees, and these jugs hang from all of them. I don't take them down until they get filled with all sorts of climbing or flying bugs.

This mixture draws them to the jug, especially when the banana peels start to rot, and the bugs climb into the jug and can't get out—and Mother Nature takes over. Approximately twice, sometimes 3 times a year, during the growing season I dump the stuff out and redo a new jug, but it catches bugs you can't imagine are even in the area, let alone chomping on your trees. I use heavy twine to wrap through the milk jug handle and then tie them onto the branches. When it comes time to dump the contents, I do so in the compost pile. After all, the bugs are nutritious and will give something back to the soil.

(Editor's Note: This will attract beneficial bugs as well as pests, so be aware of the bug harvest if you plan to do this.)

Alice Thornton
Sherwood, OR

Making Scents, Upon Reflection

Keep animals away from shrubs by spraying animal scent, available at garden centers and by mail order. Or put up a mirror near your plants. Many an animal thinks it's another animal and stays away!

Marsha A. Boinski
Ware Shoals, SC

Taking a Shine to the Birds

I like birds, but not in my garden! So I use Mylar or brightly colored plastic strips, tied all along my garden fence. The shiny fabric flaps and scares them out. It keeps birds out without harming them!

Kathleen Risk
Lafayette, IN

A Painting Genius

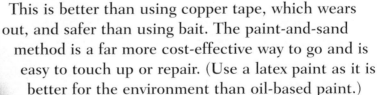

To keep snails and slugs out of a raised garden bed or container, buy some paint (any color you like) and get some sand from the sandbox or store. Paint the top edge of the raised bed or container and then sprinkle the sand on the paint while it's still wet. This creates a rough, but decorative, surface that the snails and slugs won't cross, because the surface is too rough for them to cross over.

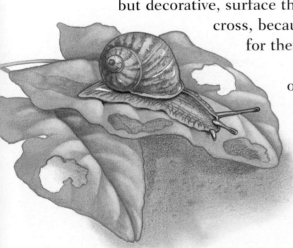

This is better than using copper tape, which wears out, and safer than using bait. The paint-and-sand method is a far more cost-effective way to go and is easy to touch up or repair. (Use a latex paint as it is better for the environment than oil-based paint.)

Stephen Sullivan
Milpitas, CA

Slip-Slidin' Away

To keep squirrels from climbing up birdfeeder posts, smear petroleum jelly on the post in an area from 2 feet to 4 feet off the ground. The squirrels find it too slippery.

Rose Anne Wheeler
Willingboro, NJ

A Shell Game for Slugs

My ducks are the best slug control. However, last year my new dog was a bit too active for the ducks, so they stayed in the barnyard and slugs grew huge in my 1-acre yard and gardens. To deter them, I took some crushed oyster shell that I had for the chickens and put it around my plants. I had very little slug damage to my garden. (I think the rough edges of the shells deter the slugs.) This year, my dog protects the ducks, so they are again on slug patrol and they don't seem to damage my plants.

Cheryl McAtee
Vancouver, WA

Canned Heat

I use the following spray to chase away all types of rodents and bugs. It's usually only necessary to spray a plant once (maybe twice if it rains immediately afterward). Caution! Do not spray directly on fruits or vegetables because it will make the fruits taste hot. Wear gloves when handling hot peppers, and don't rub your eyes!

Directions: Crush or blend up several sliced pickled jalapeño pepper rings. Place peppers and $\frac{1}{2}$ cup of the pickling juice into a spray bottle, fill the bottle with water and allow it to sit for a couple of hours. Spray plants with mixture and watch the bugs run. (It keeps rabbits at bay, too.)

Peggy Hopkins
Bay City, MI

"Dryer" Is Better

I am always looking for ways to keep the deer from eating my flowers, especially the hostas. I have had success by placing lint from the dryer under the leaves. I think there is enough human odor to keep the deer at bay. The lint is hidden under the leaves so it is not unsightly.

Therese Barry
McTaire, LA

Light-Handed Moth Control

To trap moths, place a container of water with a little mineral oil in it under a light. The moths are attracted by the light, swoop into the water and cannot get out when their wings get coated with oil. This will cut down the number of eggs laid and worms hatched.

Marie J. Hoyer
Lewistown, MT

Rubbing Out Deer

One thing we have to contend with on the farm is deer scraping their antlers on our young spruce trees and saplings. They can severely damage a tree or kill it altogether. I went around and rubbed stick deodorant all up and down the trunks of the young trees and the scent stopped the deer from scraping.

Janet Park
Oakland, MD

Editor's Tip

To minimize the likelihood that mosquitoes will be attracted to you, avoid wearing dark colors at feeding time—generally dawn and dusk. Mosquitoes are attracted to dark, moving shapes. And never wear perfume or cologne when mosquitoes are around. They love animal scents and will find you more attractive than you care to be.

Garden Seasoning

To get rid of ants and anthills, sprinkle black pepper on the hill or ant trail. The ants will not cross the pepper line. If you've got an anthill, just pour it inside there and they will be gone. It's safer than sprays, and rabbits hate it too.

Carol Frederick
Ambridge, PA

Shoe, You Deer!

I know that deer are afraid of human scent, so when I found they had visited my flower garden and eaten the flowers and buds off, I took off my old garden shoes and laid one on each end of the garden plot. I then took an old rub-on deodorant stick, opened it, and set it in the middle of the plot. Never again did another deer make munchies out of my flowers.

Janet Park
Oakland, MD

Joyful Solution for Bugs

To keep your potted plants bug free, fill a 1-gallon bucket with 1 teaspoon of liquid lemon dish soap and warm water. Use the sprayer nozzle of your kitchen sink to make a lot of suds. Set a potted plant beside the bucket and scoop the lemon soap suds onto the plant, covering top and undersides of all the leaves. Let the plant air dry. I do this twice a month, more if needed, to control whiteflies and aphids. It really works, and keeps the leaves shiny too! I use this method in our greenhouses every other week and it really keeps a handle on the bugs.

Brenda Mason
Berkeley Springs, WV

Hound-Ing the Deer

Deer are afraid of dogs, so we moved our dog and his house near the fence around the vegetable garden. One year we even borrowed our neighbor's dog. This method really keeps the deer out.

Janet Park
Oakland, MD

Editor's Tip

If you use homemade pest sprays, such as garlic spray or hot pepper spray, add a little dish soap—about a tablespoon per quart—after you blend up your spray. The dish soap helps to disperse the ingredients more evenly on plant leaves, and also helps the spray adhere. Adding it last and giving it a quick spin keeps you from having a blender full of suds.

Powdered Ant-Control

To keep ants out of the house in the warm spring weather, I sprinkle a line of Epsom salts in my windowsills. A box of Epsom salts is inexpensive and has worked for me.

Peggy Loudermilk
Granite Falls, NC

Fencing Lesson

To keep dogs or cats from digging in the garden, lay down a piece of wire fence (I used chain-link). Secure it to the ground with staples made from wire coat hangers. Plant seeds or seedlings in the openings of the fence. Plants will grow up through the openings to hide the fence. A thin layer of mulch or compost will keep the fence out of sight during the winter.

Lynn Adams
Croydon, PA

Keeping Bugs at Bay

If you scatter crushed bay leaves at the back of kitchen shelves, it will keep roaches away! Also, it will keep weevils out of dry goods, such as oatmeal, dry cereals, crackers, cornmeal, flour and macaroni. This works perfectly in dried herbs and spices. Just place a piece of dried bay leaf in each jar and I guarantee there will be no bugs.

Brenda Mason
Berkeley Springs, WV

Two Mole Removers

To get rid of moles, you must get rid of their food supply, or at least cut down the supply. Moles eat grubs and earthworms. You can keep the beneficial earthworms and destroy the grubs by applying milky spore. Another method is to get a good mouser (cat). Our cat decreased the mole supply even without having claws. He would sit in the yard at night until the moles came out to eat. Then he left his catches at the doorstep as proof of his abilities!

Peggy Loudermilk
Granite Falls, NC

Solution in a Tube

To prevent cutworms from devouring the tender young stems of my tomato and pepper plants in the spring, I place a cardboard toilet paper tube around the base of the plant. I sink half in the ground and leave half out. Partially fill the upper half with soil. There is no way the worms can get to the stems. (Paper towel tubes cut in half work too.)

Dorothy R. Raimondi
Anderson, SC

No Moths, No Squirrels

Keep pesky squirrels from digging up your prized bulbs by sprinkling the ground with moth balls (not flakes) following planting. Gently "step" them into the ground. Squirrels don't like the smell. (Original fragrance works best for me.)

S. R. Ward
South Haven, MI

Herbal Moth Repellent

Did you know that a combination of lavender, rosemary, rue, bay and cloves works well to keep away moths? Make a small bag out of cheesecloth and fill with the herbs. Hang it in a closet or place it in a drawer.

Brenda Mason
Berkeley Springs, WV

A Better Scent for Skunks

Skunks hate the smell of perfume. Douse a handful of yarn or other material with perfume, then cut the ankle and foot part of old nylon hose and stick the yarn inside. Tie a knot and place in any area skunks invade. Then no more skunks!

Marge Steinberger
Howell, MI

Ban Burrowers

Fencing is the best way to keep out larger critters. While an 8-foot fence will usually keep deer out, half that height will work for smaller pests. Bury a portion of a chicken-wire fence to frustrate burrowing animals. (You have to have a fence that they cannot crawl through.) Fold the chicken wire about six inches from the bottom and bury it to the outside of the fence, and then stake the part that is upright. This will frustrate rabbits and other burrowing critters. You can also attach sheets of plastic to the outside of the fence, as a windbreak.

Ethel Griffin
Via Email

Pest Containment

Gophers and mice love to eat tender roots and bulbs. The best way we've found to protect bulbs and small shrubs from burrowing critters is to plant in containers buried the proper depth and big enough to allow for growth. Example: small pots for clumps of bulbs; and washtubs, horse troughs, etc. for lilacs and other small shrubs. The county dump has a treasure of old rusty items; holes for drainage are already there!

Mr. & Mrs. Donald D. Hastings
Lookout, CA

Editor's Tip

Clean your birdbath at least every week. Use 9 parts water to 1 part household bleach and give the bath a good scrubbing. This makes for a healthier drinking and bathing area for birds. (The bleach will evaporate quickly and be harmless.)

Beat the Beetles

Last year we had a problem with cucumber beetles here in Maine. Our beautiful cucumber and squash seedlings suddenly started to shrivel up and die. Close examination revealed the culprits. We tried all organic remedies such as dusting with cayenne mix, soapy pepper spray, etc. The beetles just flew off to return later.

So we developed the following two-part method. Very early in the morning the beetles are sluggish. During this time you can scoop them up with a plastic spoon from inside the blossoms where they tend to aggregate in the nectar, and pick them off of the leaves. The collected bugs can be crushed with a rock or drowned in a jar of soapy water.

If you don't like to get up early and put in the effort you can resort to the second part alone. This is where you put your neighborhood birds to work. We had put up stakes in the garden to support garden peas. We noticed that birds would perch on these stakes and frequently dive down onto the squash plants. Upon closer watch we found out they were able to see the beetles hovering around the squash plants from these perches and were feeding on them. So we collected old tree branches that provided ideal perches for the birds and stuck them near all squash plants. It worked beautifully. Our plants recovered and we had all sorts of squash and cukes. We also had hours of fun watching the birds from our window doing the beetle eradication for us. No chemicals needed!

(Editor's Note: Floating row covers are another option for controlling cucumber beetles, but they need to be removed once plants bloom to let pollinators in.)

Rosy Chacko
Winslow, ME

High-Fat Rabbit Diet

I have a method for keeping the rabbits out of the garden that is simple and costs next to nothing. All you need are some foot-long stakes, some string or twine, and some lard or frying fat (I use the grease that comes out of bacon or ham when you fry it).

Push the stakes in the ground and space them so that they will hold the string or twine about 6 inches off the ground around the garden, around a single row, or around a few plants. Then grease the string with the lard or fat. The rabbits don't like the scent and will not bother your garden.

Russell Deorazio
Schenectady, NY

Rub It in Against Aphids

Almost every gardener has dealt with aphids. When my plants are attacked by aphids, I fight back with a natural control: Take 4 ounces of rubbing alcohol and dilute with 32 ounces of water. Add 1 teaspoon of dish soap. (Be sure to add dish soap last and shake well before using.) Spray your plants as needed. Note: Do not exceed ratio of rubbing alcohol to water because alcohol can burn foliage if not diluted properly.

Susan Hilbert
Reno, NV

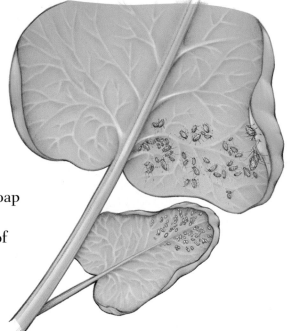

Hot Stuff

You can make your own critter repellent by mixing 2 tablespoons hot pepper sauce with 1 tablespoon liquid soap, plus 1 teaspoon garlic powder, to 1 gallon water. You have to repeat after rainfall, but otherwise you should spray every 2 to 4 weeks.

Ethel Griffin
Via Email

A Catty Approach

I have five outside cats. The way I keep them out of the beds, pots and containers is by using plastic forks. I put the handles in the ground with the tines sticking up, a few inches apart. The forks won't disturb newly planted seeds or young plants. When the plants grow bigger the forks are hidden. They can also be used again the next year.

Mary Hall
Caddo, OK

Hose Off Those Moths

To keep moths out of cabbage plants, stretch a net of pantyhose over the entire plant, or use a small mesh net.

Donna King
Lake Butler, FL

Smelling Like a Rose

We have had trouble with our farm cats wanting to dig against the house in winter to do their bathroom jobs. The smell was awful in spring and summer when we wanted to have the windows open. So the next fall and spring when we pruned our roses, we put all the prunings against the house over the soft dirt. The cats felt the thorns and decided it wasn't worth the effort to dig there anymore.

Valerie Giesbrecht
Othello, WA

Editor's Tip

It may be hard to believe at times, but humans aren't the first food choice of mosquitoes. They prefer to feed on small mammals—rabbits, squirrels, deer, and so forth. Why does this matter? Well, your dog and cat are small mammals. If your pets are out a lot, don't let them suffer with lots of bites. And get both dogs and cats checked for heartworm, which can be a result of mosquito bites.

Scratch One Raccoon

I keep raccoons out of my sweet corn patch by planting pumpkins and winter squash between the rows. Raccoons don't like the scratchy leaves. Plus, I get a double-duty harvest.

Alice R. Nelson
Beloit, WI

Rabbits on the Net

After fighting to save my tender annuals every spring from those cute but pesky rabbits, I discovered that bird netting was my answer. I took the netting used to keep birds out of fruit trees and discovered that it works on rabbits also. Just cut a square foot of it and cut a hole in the center of the square just big enough to place over your newly transplanted annuals or perennials. Secure one or more of the edges with a small amount of dirt or stone. The rabbits will not walk on the netting.

I was losing several annuals each week until I implemented this idea. I didn't loose another plant the rest of the summer. It actually even frustrated those gregarious grackles and other feathered "friends."

Kathryn Palmer
Canton, IL

Fighting Fire Ants

I've had success with this homemade organic fire ant control: Make a concentrate of equal parts of citrus oil, compost tea and molasses. Mix the concentrate with approximately 1 gallon of water. To use, carefully dig into a fire ant mound with a garden fork and quickly drench with 1 to 2 ounces of solution. We find this works as well as any chemical control and nourishes the soil at the same time. (Be careful not to disturb fire ants when applying, or they will attack!) Always wear protective clothing when around fire ants.

Pat Hayton
Grand Prairie, TX

Turn, Turn, Turn the Birds Away

Hang compact discs with nylon thread or monofilament line to keep birds out of the garden. Discs sparkle in sunlight or daylight with any slight movement. Birds dislike it and stay away.

Lloyd J. Baudier
Kenner, LA

Give Deer Enough Rope

There is a serious deer problem here in the Poconos. They eat almost everything and anything. My 4-foot garden fence is not high enough to keep deer out, so my husband put pole extensions every 5 feet on the fence. Then we strung a heavy yellow rope around the top. The deer sense the rope there and are afraid to jump in. My vegetables are safe inside the ropes. The only cost is for the ropes!

Rita von Schwedler
Tannersville, PA

Editor's Tip

If an 8-foot deer fence is out of the question, try setting up a 5-foot one with a hedge of evergreens a few feet inside of the fence. The deer can't leap that great a distance, and you'll have the added benefit of year-round greenery.

Exhausting the Deer

To keep deer from my tasty rhododendron plants, I planted them near my dryer exhaust. It doesn't harm the plants, but the smell from the dryer will drive the deer away. I haven't had one nibble in 3 years on the plants near the dryer exhaust!

Kate Lee
Swiftwater, PA

Fruitful Fixes

I have a small orchard of 40 trees. To trap fruit flies, I paint fish bobbers red, then coat them with tree "stickem" and hang them in trees. Also, I mix 1 tablespoon of molasses with 3 cups of apple cider vinegar, put it in containers, and hang them in apple trees for moths and flies.

William Fugitt
Flat Rock, MI

Playing Chicken with Pests

I had a problem with the local wild critters eating my newly planted bulbs. I think I solved the problem this past fall. I bought a roll of chicken wire 36 inches wide and cut it into 18-inch strips. Next, I dug holes 18 x 18 inches and about 2 inches deeper than the bulb's planting level. I put down one end of the chicken wire in the hole and bend up the other end. I then fill in about 2 inches of the hole with dirt and place the bulbs. I fill the hole to about $1\frac{1}{2}$ to 2 inches from the top, fold over the chicken wire and fill in the rest of the hole. The neighborhood critters have attempted to dig up the bulbs, but can't get through the chicken wire. I made sure to leave plenty of room for the bulbs to divide and spread.

Maureen D. Goodwin
Framingham, MA

A "Cheep" Hot Tub

I have a bird-lover's tip. I used to put away my birdbath every September and begin to use it again in May. This year I wanted to buy a heater cable for it for year-round use, but the heater cost too much. Now I take a bucket of hot water and "pop" out the small layer of ice in the mornings and replace with fresh water. The birds are grateful, and I even caught deer drinking from the birdbath!

Rita von Schwedler
Tannersville, PA

Editor's Tip

If you're troubled with English sparrows eating your preferred birds' food, give the sparrows their own feeding area. They prefer to eat off the ground, so scatter white millet—a favorite sparrow food—on an area away from your other feeders. (Be sure this area is several feet away from cover where cats and other predators can hide.)

Thumper-Thwarters

I soak cotton balls with garlic oil/juice and attached them to my roses to keep the rabbits from nibbling on young rose plants in the spring. I have also used cat hair hung in mesh bags. Both work very well against rabbits.

Pamela Morrison
Dearborn, MI

Unwinding in the Garden

We found a way to harvest our cherries instead of turning them all over to the birds. I use pieces of old black garden hose elsewhere in the garden to discourage the birds. So I thought I would try hanging something dark in the cherry tree. Since the tree is small and hose is heavy, we took an old cassette tape instead and threw it back and forth over the tree, so it unwound and looped over the branches. One tape covered the tree sufficiently and even a slight breeze set the strips writhing and moving. The plastic strips must have looked "snake-like" to the birds because we reaped a plentiful harvest for family, friends and our own supply.

M. Wise
Tiffin, OH

Deer-Repellent Fabric

From a fabric store, I purchase the least expensive nylon netting available. In the fall, after the ground freezes, I load my garden sled with a bucket of snap-on clothes pins, netting and large shears. Then I set out to prepare deciduous trees

and bushes for the onslaught of deer roaming our land all season. I place a piece of netting over the bush large enough to generously cover the bush, secure the netting with a few clothes pins, and I have the bush protected for the entire season against the nibbling of deer.

Alice McConnell
Ely, MN

Branching Out with the Birds

Here's how I increase my bird visits. I live in the mountains in Southern California with forests all around. Off my bedroom is a small deck from which I like to watch the birds. I hang several feeders, waterers and hummingbird feeders in season, but I noticed there weren't many places for the birds to perch and socialize. So I found some downed branches in the woods and placed them (artistically) in the railings of the deck, creating artificial "trees." The birds just loved it!

Since I also wanted to hide some power lines from view, I added some pine and spruce branches that had fallen, to the mix. Not only do the birds love it, providing a more natural habitat for them, but it really helps to block unsightly wires and give me a little privacy and a nicer view. I think this has increased bird visitations 100 percent!

Kathleen Brown
Green Valley Lake, CA

Just a Little Over the Ears...

I've had good luck using hair to keep my sweet corn safe. After my corn has tasseled and set ears, I spread hair through the rows and sprinkle it around on the plants. I believe it helps keep the raccoons out. I also read that hair keeps deer out, too. When I have an appointment to get my hair cut, I ask my beautician to save me other customers' hair, too.

Jeanne Kerwood
Bruning, NE

This "Suets" Their Appetite

An easy way to attract birds to your yard is with suet. I've found a very easy way to make my own, and the birds love it. Simply take a small aluminum pie pan (the kind frozen pot pies come in) and fill it about halfway with bird seed. Then, after frying bacon, sausage or hamburgers, just drain the fat off the meat into the seed-filled pie pan. Place it in the freezer overnight. Remove the contents from the pie pan and place it outside. Your birds will be thrilled! You can also add raisins or any kind of nuts to this.

Marlon Evans
Winston-Salem, NC

Group Therapy

To attract more butterflies and hummingbirds to our gardens last year, we grouped bee balm (*Monarda*) with our butterfly bush and *Coreopsis* 'Moonbeam'. What a delight it was to see the fluttering creatures gather around my beautiful perennial gardens!

LuAnne Sadowski
Kennedy, NY

A Homemade Pooper-Scooper

Here's how to be ready for the occasional dog that wanders into your yard and leaves an unwanted "package." Make a scoop from a plastic gallon jug with the bottom cut out of it. It works fine for picking up and disposing of the whole works, and has a handle. The jug may be washed and ready for the next visit.

Betsy Kalkwarf
Richland, WA

Making a Splash

Birds and butterflies like dripping water, so here's an inexpensive way to provide it. Take a garden pole with a hook and an old bucket with a handle. Put a pinhole in the bottom of the bucket. Then put a rock (or birdbath) under the bucket. (If you use a rock, it needs to be flat with a small dip in the center to hold water.) The drips from the bucket will make the water move, and if the water makes mud around the rock the butterflies will love it.

Kelly Blodgett
Winter, WI

Mad About Mud

When planning a butterfly garden, don't forget to provide a puddle for the butterflies. A shallow flowerpot saucer filled with sand or soil and water does nicely.

Diana Smith
Kelso, WA

Healthy Plants, Happy Harvests

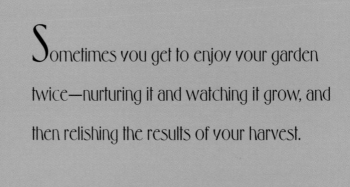

Sometimes you get to enjoy your garden twice—nurturing it and watching it grow, and then relishing the results of your harvest.

Here are members' best ideas for making sure you get the results you want from your vegetables and herbs (and more). Plus you'll find superb recipes, also from members, for preparing your garden's bounty in the kitchen.

Ripeness Rites

Here's how I've learned to tell when produce is ripe:

Snap Beans: Examine the point that extends beyond the body of the bean. If the protrusion is curved or limp, the bean will produce a satisfying snap. If the protrusion is straight and rigid, there will be a string.

Cantaloupes: The "belly button" should be slightly soft. If the melon is soft all over, then it's probably too ripe.

Lemons: Lemons with the smoothest skin and the smallest points on each end will usually have the most juice and best flavor.

Radishes: When the crop is ready for harvest, these fleshy roots will often thrust themselves slightly up above the ground.

Squash: For the tenderest squash, harvest when the blossom at the end of the fruit is about to disappear.

Rhonda Watson
Reedley, CA

A Green Bean Haircut

After green beans stop producing the first crop, cut them back to 3 to 4 inches high. Fertilize and water well, and the plants will regrow and produce another crop.

Marie J. Hoyer
Lewistown, MT

Seed Storage in 32 Flavors

To store my seeds after harvesting, I save 5-quart ice cream buckets. They're easy to fill, and label easily with a marker pen. I use a pushpin to put holes in the lid. (I make sure the seeds are well dried before storing.) I store the seeds in my laundry room. To conserve energy, we close the laundry room doors so the room is cool and dry.

Darlene B. Thomas
Double Springs, AL

RECIPE:
RICE-STUFFED PORK CHOPS

4 extra-thick pork chops (1$\frac{1}{2}$ inches)

$\frac{1}{2}$ cup cooked rice (brown or white)

1 clove garlic, minced or pressed

$\frac{1}{2}$ tsp. dried marjoram leaves

$\frac{1}{4}$ tsp. salt

2 T. olive or salad oil

1$\frac{1}{2}$ cups dry white wine or chicken broth

$\frac{3}{4}$ cup whipped cream

1 T. green peppercorns or capers

2 tomatoes for garnish

Parsley for garnish

Cut a pocket in each pork chop with tip of sharp knife. Mix rice, garlic, marjoram and salt. Divide mixture among chops. Pack into chops well.

Heat oil in heavy skillet. Slowly brown chops on both sides. Add wine/broth. Cover; simmer 30 minutes. Remove chops; keep warm. Boil liquid in pan down to about $\frac{1}{2}$ cup (it should appear thickened and glossy).

Stir in cream and peppercorns/capers. Boil 3 to 5 minutes until thickened. Pour over pork chops or serve separately in a bowl. Garnish chops with tomato halves and parsley. Serve immediately.

Serves 4.

Victoria Mongeon
Park River, ND

Flavorful Again

Revive the flavor of dried herbs by soaking them in 1 teaspoon of lemon juice or vinegar for about 10 minutes before using.

Brenda Mason
Berkeley Springs, WV

Recipe:
Chicken Delight

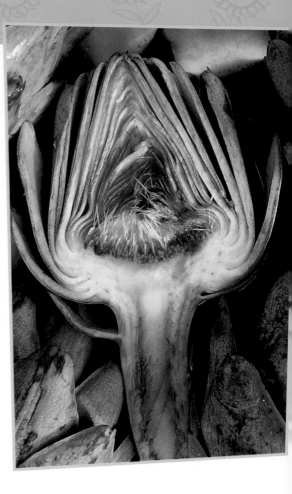

4 to 6 boneless, skinless chicken breast halves

1 can artichoke hearts, drained, halved

2 T. dried, chopped tomatoes

1½ cups coarsely chopped red or green cabbage

1 medium tomato, chopped

1 T. cooking wine (white or red)

Salt to taste

Pepper to taste

Pinch of dried, hot peppers (optional)

2 cups water

Roll chicken in flour. Heat olive oil in skillet; brown chicken. Add all other ingredients. Simmer for 1 hour. Serve over rice or noodles.

Diana L. Slone
Galion, OH

Horseradish without Tears

Dig horseradish roots, cut off the tops, then wash them thoroughly with the garden hose. Put the roots into your washing machine and wash them as if they were a load of clothes—except you don't need soap. Then remove the roots and wipe out the washing machine tub.

Cut any bad or soft spots and sort the roots into small, medium and large sizes. Prepare each size separately in your blender. Cut up the roots if needed, and add enough white vinegar so they can be pureed. Add salt to taste, and pour into containers and keep in the refrigerator. These are great for holiday gifts. (Editor's Note: Be careful when you open the blender lid. The fumes can be strong!)

Ardith Morton
Merriman, NE

Editor's Tip

If your flowering shrubs bloom before the strawberries are ripe, prune them right away after blooming. (Examples are lilac, forsythia, mock orange and some azaleas.) Those shrubs that flower after the strawberry season are best pruned in early spring. If you need to do heavy pruning, stagger the pruning over a couple of years so you still get bloom.

Cute Idea for Cukes

To make ripening and harvesting of cucumbers a little easier, I use "miniature fence" edging as supports under the plants. I use old wooden ones that no longer serve a decorative purpose. I place the fences at different angles throughout the rows and growing areas. As the plants grow vines I lay them over the fence. When cukes grow, the fruits are lifted off the dirt a little so they don't get yellow spots. Plus, they're easier to pick.

Cara McIlquham
Chippewa Falls, WI

Editor's Tip

If you want to know how much water to give your lawn, try this: Place a rain gauge or shallow pan on the grass and water the lawn until there's an inch of water in the pan or gauge. Wait an hour or two, then dig into the root zone of a part of the lawn. See how deeply the water has penetrated (generally, the deeper, the better unless you have very porous soil). If the water hasn't gone very deep, consider aerating your lawn or amending the soil with organic matter for better drainage. Checking moisture penetration this way is a good technique everywhere in the garden. You might be surprised to see the results.

Don't Stack the Odds

A trick to collecting ripe tomatoes is to place them in a single layer. Do not pile them up on top of each other, because they bruise very easily. The bottom part of a seed-starting tray makes a very good tomato-picking tray.

Arnold & Carol Shaw
No. Berwick, ME

RECIPE: ROSE PETAL JELLY

Rose petals

4 cups apple juice

1 T. margarine

1 pkg. Surejell

4¼ cups sugar

To make infusion of rose petals: Fill saucepan with fresh, clean, chemical-free rose petals. Cover petals with water. Bring to a boil; cook for about 10 minutes. Strain, saving liquid.

In a large stockpot, place 2 cups rose water infusion, apple juice and margarine. Combine Surejell with ¼ cup sugar; add to mixture. Bring to a rolling boil, stirring constantly. Add remaining 4 cups sugar, stirring constantly. Return to rolling boil; cook for 2 to 3 minutes, stirring constantly. Remove from heat, skim any foam from top and pour into sterilized canning jars. Seal according to jar directions or with melted paraffin. Takes 2 to 3 weeks to set properly.

Nada Fisher
Longmont, CO

The "10-Minute Herb Rack"

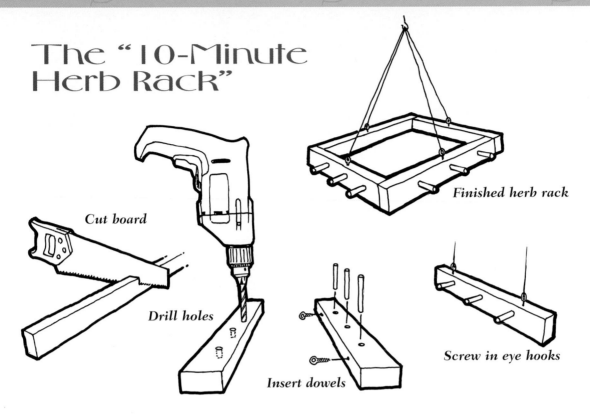

Cut board

Drill holes

Insert dowels

Finished herb rack

Screw in eye hooks

MATERIALS REQUIRED:

$\frac{1}{4}$- or $\frac{3}{8}$-inch wooden dowel

1 x 2- or 2 x 2-foot wooden board

Wood glue

Screw-in eye hooks

Sandpaper

TOOLS REQUIRED:

Saw (or have the dowels and wood board precut to size at the store)

Drill and drill bit to match dowel size

Staple gun; wood screws or nails (optional, used to build variations of basic rack)

ASSEMBLY DIRECTIONS:

Cut the board into 2-foot sections or any desired length. Next cut the dowel into 2-inch sections. Sand the rough cut edges with medium-grit sandpaper. Next drill holes about 6 inches deep. You can put a piece of tape on the drill bit at $\frac{1}{2}$ inch to guide your hole depth while drilling.

Next, put a little wood glue into each hole and insert the dowels. Allow time to dry. Screw in the eye hooks if you intend to hang the rack from the ceiling, otherwise you can nail or screw it directly into the wall.

You can stain it, paint it or leave it natural. When you harvest your herbs, tie them in bunches at the stem using raffia, hemp cord or rubber bands. Hang the herbs on the protruding dowels and allow them to dry. It's simple, effective and attractive!

Marshall R. Pilcher
Antioch, TN

RECIPE:
CARNITAS
A WONDERFUL SOUTH-OF-THE-BORDER PORK ENTRÉE

Pork butt roast (any size)	Tomatoes
Cumin powder	Onion
Garlic powder	Avocado
Onion powder	Fresh lemon
Salt	Fresh lime
Pepper	Flour tortillas
Cilantro	Salsa

Preheat oven to 450°F.

Simmer pork in water on low heat until it falls apart. Add cumin, garlic and onion powders, salt, pepper and cilantro.

Remove pork from water. Shred and place in roasting pan. Season with more cumin, garlic and onion powders, salt, pepper and cilantro. Bake for approximately 20 minutes (until a little crunchy on top).

Cut up tomato, onion and avocado for garnishing; serve on large platter with lemon and lime wedges. Serve carnitas in warm tortillas; top with salsa.

Linda B. Williams
Pinnacle, NC

Timing Is Everything

Always cut leafy herbs for drying early in the day before the sun gets too hot, but after the dew has dried on the foliage. The oil content is higher at that time.

Brenda Mason
Berkeley Springs, WV

Take It Outside

At harvest time, we process a lot of vegetables. When possible, we like to do the messy stuff outside and don't have to worry about the drips and splashes. Our picnic table under a big old cherry tree is an ideal spot. We just hose everything clean when we're finished.

M. Wise
Tiffin, OH

A Freewheeling Bean Tepee

I have a great technique for pole beans. First, I set a 10-foot PVC pipe securely in the ground. Then I take an old bicycle wheel and bolt a 6- or 8-inch metal rod to the axle. Then I lay the bicycle wheel on top of the PVC pipe. The rod fits inside the pipe to stabilize the wheel.

Next I attached several strings of baling twine to the outer edge of the wheel, leaving each twine long enough to reach the ground with a little extra for slack to tie to a stake. I plant my beans in a circle around the PVC pipe, out away from the pipe so that the twines will be at an angle from the ground to the bicycle wheel. I put a stake in the ground where beans are planted and secure the strings to the stakes.

The first time I tried this, my beans grew to the top of the twines. When I could no longer reach the topmost beans, I used a stepladder. By having a little slack in the strings, I was able to turn the bicycle wheel enough each way so that I could pick those at the top without having to keep moving my ladder.

Martha J. Kehr
East Otto, NY

An Idea with Legs

To keep cabbage worms off of broccoli, cut pieces of pantyhose big enough to slip over broccoli heads when small and tie both ends. The nylon will stretch as the heads grow. No more cabbage worms!

Alice R. Nelson
Beloit, WI

RECIPE:
BRUSCHETTA WITH FRESH TOMATOES AND GARLIC

1 1/2 lbs. ripe, juicy tomatoes

8 slices crusty Italian bread, cut 1/2 inch thick

1 to 2 cloves garlic, minced

1 to 2 T. capers, rinsed and patted dry

1/4 cup loosely packed, fresh oregano or 10 to 12 fresh basil leaves, shredded

Salt

Freshly ground pepper

1/3 cup extra virgin olive oil

Bring a medium-sized saucepan of water to a boil. Cut a cross at root end of tomatoes and drop them into boiling water. Cook until skin of tomatoes begins to split; 1 to 2 minutes. Put tomatoes in a bowl of ice water. Peel, seed and coarsely chop tomatoes. Place them in a strainer and let drain over a bowl for 20 minutes to allow tomatoes to release all juices.

Brush bread with olive oil; place on grill or under broiler until golden brown on both sides. Note: Watch the bread very carefully so it doesn't burn.

Put the tomatoes, garlic, capers and oregano/basil in a bowl. Season with salt and pepper to taste. Add olive oil; mix well. Spoon tomato mixture onto bread and serve.

Donna R. Dankoff
Kouts, IN

Keep 'em Coming

To get the most out of a small space, plant leaf lettuce, radishes and broccoli in the same row. Harvest radishes first, lettuce second and broccoli third. You can reseed the radishes and lettuce for a continued harvest, too.

Susan Holster
Newton, AL

RECIPE: HOMEMADE PESTO

1 cup fresh basil leaves,
firmly packed

$\frac{1}{2}$ cup grated Parmesan cheese

Salt

$\frac{1}{2}$ cup parsley

$\frac{1}{4}$ cup pine nuts or walnuts

2 cloves garlic, chopped

$\frac{1}{2}$ cup olive oil

Puree basil, Parmesan cheese, salt, parsley, pine nuts/walnuts and garlic in blender or food processor. With machine running, slowly add oil and blend until smooth. Makes about 1 cup.

Jean Flipse
East Islip, NY

RECIPE: SPICY PEPPER SOUP

4 sweet red peppers

1 small sweet yellow pepper

3 large red cherry peppers

2 red jalapeño peppers

2 large cloves garlic

1 can chicken broth

Fresh basil leaves (optional topping)

Sour cream (optional topping)

Slice and seed peppers; remove membranes. Place in microwave; cook for 5 minutes. Run garlic cloves through food processor; chop well. In saucepan, add peppers and garlic to chicken broth; bring to a boil. Simmer until well blended; about 20 minutes. Serve with garnish of fresh basil or a swirl of sour cream.

Toni Sweeney
Kearney, NE

Bunches
Of Beauty

For beautiful dried
peonies: Just as the flower
is about half open, I cut the
stems, taking enough for a
bouquet. I cluster a half
dozen or so peonies
together and wrap a rubber
band a few inches down on
the stems. Then I hang
them upside down over the clothesline in
my cool, dark basement until they are
completely dried. These peonies are great
for dried arrangements!

Harriet Link
Renville, MN

Editor's
Tip

If you have freezing winters
and grow evergreens, water
them well in the fall up
until freezing. This will
help them survive the
winter, because the
evergreens can't absorb
water from the roots when
the ground is frozen.
Watering during prolonged
thaws is a good idea too.

A Peachy
Picking Idea

For years, my husband and I
have had a peach tree loaded with the most delicious
peaches I have ever eaten. But it was so tall we couldn't
reach the ones in the top of the tree and kept losing those
goodies when they would fall to the ground and burst. But
we figured out an easy way to pick them.

My husband got a long, thin pole and nailed a big coffee
can on the end. (We removed the top but left the bottom on.)
Then we could stand on the ground, stick the can under a big
juicy peach, and wiggle the pole a little. The peach would drop into the can, and we
could bring it down to eye level and lay a perfect peach into the basket.

Jean H. Goddard
Bowling Green, KY

Recipe: Italian Stacked Chicken with Tomato Pesto Pasta

Italian Stacked Chicken

2 T. extra virgin olive oil

1 to 2 scallions, diced

3 chicken breasts, boneless

2 stems fresh oregano
(or $^3/_4$ tsp. dried oregano)

$^1/_2$ lb. prosciutto, thinly sliced

$^1/_2$ lb. provolone, sliced

Preheat oven to 360°F.

Pour oil into skillet; cook over medium-high heat. Add scallions; cook until browned. Add chicken and oregano; cook through. Place cooked chicken into casserole dish. Starting with prosciutto, place 2 layers of meat and cheese on each side of breast. (Chicken can also be stuffed.) Bake until cheese is slightly browned (about 15 minutes).

Tomato Pesto Pasta

1 box penne pasta

$^1/_3$ cup olive oil

2 cloves garlic

3 T. flour

3 tomatoes, cubed

$^1/_2$ cup chopped fresh parsley

$^1/_2$ cup chopped fresh basil

$^1/_2$ cup grated Romano cheese

$^1/_4$ cup nuts of choice
(walnuts, pine nuts, etc.)

Cook pasta; drain. Heat oil in skillet; lightly brown garlic. Flour tomatoes; cook in oil for 10 minutes, stirring constantly. Add herbs; cook 1 minute. Add cheese and nuts; cook for 2 minutes. Turn off heat; toss in pasta. Also great with olives.

Kayla Warner
Bethlehem, PA

Leaf 'em Tender

To raise good blanched cauliflower: After it heads up, grasp the long leaves and attach them over the head with a clothespin to keep the sun out.

Walter L. Balsley Jr.
Weems, VA

Prearranged Perfection

Take the time to arrange your everlasting flowers before you hang them upside down to dry. This works especially well for small arrangements and nosegays.

Carole Kopietz
Norfolk, NE

Editor's Tip

Compost—What DOESN'T Go In

Material	Problem
Meat scraps, bones or fat	Attracts rodents and other pests.
Diseased plant debris	Can spread garden diseases.
Pesticide-treated plants or wood	May kill beneficial organisms.
Noxious weeds or weeds that have set seed	Can spread into garden.
Charcoal ashes	Much too alkaline.
Pet droppings	Often contain parasites.

When Less Becomes More

Every gardener I know complains of being overwhelmed with an abundance of cucumbers, yellow crookneck squash and zucchini. After 52 years of gardening, I have solved that problem. Plant fewer, and pick them every day—sometimes twice a day—when they are very small. (Do this even if your husband keeps telling you it's wasteful to pick them so small.)

You don't have to sort and throw away any overripe and overgrown veggies. The young ones are twice as yummy with fewer and smaller seeds, so you really enjoy using them. And, with this approach you won't get to the point that you never want to see another cucumber, squash or zucchini!

Jean H. Goddard
Bowling Green, KY

Worming Out of the Work

I love beautiful flowers, but don't have the time or patience to have a compost bin. So I formed a partnership with a great group of earthworms. I now put my food scraps, vegetable trimmings, etc., directly into the ground in my flower bed and yard. The worms turn my scraps into a rich earth that produces huge flowers. Now compost bin tending, and turning, is handled directly by my "wonder worms."

Linda Walls
Edmond, OK

Some Good News About Weeds

Whenever I create a new flower bed, after I have prepared the soil, I place a layer or two of newspaper down over the entire bed, then wet it thoroughly. I cover the bed with mulch, then simply plant my favorite flowers. I have found this to be a very effective way to really reduce the weeds that can overtake a bed.

Marlon Evans
Winston-Salem, NC

The Right Solution

Here's how to use a hose-end sprayer and not mix more chemicals than you need—for example, if you want to spray five bushes with an insecticide but you don't know how much solution to make. First, spray your bushes with just water while timing yourself. Next, take a gallon bucket and time how long it takes your sprayer to fill the bucket. Now, compare the time it took to spray your bushes with the time it takes your sprayer to spray the gallon, and you now know how many gallons of solution it will take to spray your bushes. (Remember always to read the label.)

Mix only the amount you will need following the manufacturer's directions, and you should have enough to spray your bushes without having to store any extra chemicals that can pose a danger to you, your family or pets. Remember to always use a different sprayer for fertilizers and insecticides from the one you use for herbicides, or you may accidently kill plants that you wanted to keep.

Robin Nordstrom
Ellettsville, IN

Bright Bed Sheets

When making a new perennial bed, I first prepare the soil. Next I cover the bed with an old cotton sheet. Then I cover the sheet lightly with mulch, and plant as usual. The sheet does a great job of keeping weeds out, and it rots away as the perennials grow.

Rebecca J. Gervais
Moosup, CT

She Can Handle It

I found a simple way to grow dipper gourds with long handles. I grew some gourd plants on the ground and trained some others to climb my barn wall. The dipper gourds that climbed up the barn wall and hung down from the vines had necks that were long and straight. The necks of the ones grown lying on the ground grew short and curled.

Janet Park
Oakland, MD

RECIPE:
3-WAY HERB BREAD
CAN BE MADE INTO LOAVES, BREADSTICKS OR FOCACCIA

1 pkg. yeast

1 1/2 cups warm water

8 T. olive oil

4 cups flour

1/2 cup chopped green olives

1/2 cup chopped black olives (optional)

2 cloves garlic, chopped

1 T. chopped fresh rosemary

2 T. chopped fresh oregano

2 T. chopped fresh basil

Cornmeal for dusting

Dissolve yeast in water; let sit for 10 minutes. Add remaining ingredients. Knead; cover and let rise 1 hour in a warm place. Sprinkle cornmeal on work surface and roll out dough. Place in loaf pan or roll into 3-inch-long ropes and roll onto pan. Brush with olive oil; cook 12 to 15 minutes at 400°F.

If you make focaccia (back to the garden for picking!), top with more fresh basil, fresh garden tomatoes (sliced very thin), fresh broccoli (chopped), and sprinkle with mozzarella, Parmesan, and Romano cheese.

After baking you can easily freeze these breads. Just thaw and serve when needed.

Yolanda Schumacher
Circleville, OH

Editor's Tip

When pruning or snipping branches, twigs or leaves, carry a cup with a solution of one part chlorine bleach to nine parts water. Add a dash of dish soap if you wish. Then dip your pruner or cutting tool into the mixture between cuttings. This helps prevent the spread of disease from one plant to another.

RECIPE: ROASTED TOMATO SOUP

3 lbs. tomatoes, cored

1/3 cup olive oil, divided

6 cloves garlic, minced

2 T. chopped thyme

2 cups chopped onion

1/4 cup chopped basil

2 cups chicken broth

1/2 cup half-and-half

Salt to taste

Pepper to taste

Place tomatoes in a roasting pan; drizzle with 1/4 cup oil. Sprinkle garlic and thyme over tomatoes. Bake, uncovered at 350°F for 1 hour, turning occasionally.

In a large saucepan, sauté onion in remaining oil. Add tomato mixture and basil; cook for 5 minutes. Add broth; boil for 5 minutes. Put through sieve or food mill; return to pan. Warm half-and-half; stir into soup. Season with salt and pepper according to taste.

Serves 6.

Katelynn Wilcher
Mooresville, IN

Editor's Tip

If you let people smoke in your garden, be sure they don't touch plants without washing their hands. Otherwise they could spread tobacco mosaic virus (TMV) onto tomatoes, squash, and other plants.

Editor's Tip

Understanding Soil Type and Character

Soil is composed of four main elements: mineral matter, water, air and organic matter. Grains of sand, finely pulverized rock or pebbles are mineral matter. The size, proportions and type of mineral matter give the soil its basic texture, which determines its type. Broadly defined, the four soil types are sand, silt, loam and clay.

- Sandy soil is light and easy to dig, warms quickly in the spring and is rich in oxygen. However, sandy soil doesn't hold much moisture or many plant nutrients. Amendments of organic matter help sandy soils.

- Silty soil has a lighter texture than clay but is heavier than sand. Small silt particles travel easily in water, so soil in low places near rivers and streams often has a silty character. Poor drainage and surface crusting are the main problems you will have when gardening in silty soil.

- Loam is the term used to describe soil with a good balance of clay, silt and sand, and a generous amount of organic matter. It is the type of soil everyone wants to have.

- Clay soil is heavy and difficult to dig and has little pore space for oxygen. Clay often contains plenty of plant nutrients, but the nutrients may be not be available to plants because of the soil's tight texture. Clay soil tends to stay wet for a long time after heavy rains, and may drain poorly. When clay dries out it becomes rock hard. It is encouraging to know that clay soil becomes terrific garden soil if a sufficient amount of organic matter is added.

Save That Water!

Chlorinated and commercially softened water from home water softeners can ring the death knell for plants. I follow nature and put a large trash bag in my old galvanized garbage can, wire the bag just below the rim of the can and set the can under a downspout from the eaves of my house.

For indoor gardeners who have downspouts which drain near the ground, cut off the downspout 3 to 4 feet higher than the ground. Under it, set a large container to catch rainwater. The cut-off spout may be put back on the longer downspout when no longer in use.

I have cleaned and saved many gallon bleach and milk jugs, and fill them with rain water. They are ready to use when my indoor plants need watering.

Elinor Brown
Ceresco, NE

RECIPE:
PUMPKIN RIBBON BREAD

FILLING:

2 (3-oz.) pkgs. cream cheese, softened

$\frac{1}{3}$ cup sugar

1 T. flour

1 egg

2 tsp. grated orange peel

BREAD:

1 cup pumpkin, cooked

$\frac{1}{2}$ cup vegetable oil

2 eggs

$1\frac{1}{2}$ cups sugar

$\frac{1}{2}$ tsp. salt

$\frac{1}{2}$ tsp. ground cloves

$\frac{1}{2}$ tsp. cinnamon

$1\frac{2}{3}$ cups all-purpose flour

1 tsp. baking soda

1 cup chopped pecans (optional)

To prepare filling: Beat cream cheese, sugar and flour together in a small bowl. Add egg; mix to blend. Stir in orange peel; set aside.

To prepare bread: Combine pumpkin, oil and eggs in a large bowl. Add sugar, salt, cloves, cinnamon, flour, baking soda and pecans; mix to blend. Pour $\frac{1}{4}$ of the batter into two greased and floured $7\frac{1}{2}$- x $3\frac{1}{2}$- x 3-inch loaf pans. Carefully spread the cream cheese mixture over bread batter. Add remaining bread batter, covering filling. Bake at 325°F for $1\frac{1}{2}$ hours, or until bread tests done with toothpick. Cool 10 minutes before removing from pans. Store bread in refrigerator.

Tracy Rodenbach
Liberty, KY

A Crate Idea for Bulbs

When storing gladiolus bulbs for winter, I use a plastic milk crate. I put newspaper on the bottom, then partially fill the case with clean bulbs. I put the bulbs in an unheated room. The milk crate allows ventilation and is easily transported.

Kathie Means
New Lisbon, WI

RECIPE: SALSA

2½ qts. tomatoes, peeled, chopped	½ cup cider vinegar
2 cups chopped onions	4 tsp. salt
½ cup chopped bell peppers	1 T. garlic powder
½ cup chopped jalapeño peppers (use more if peppers are too mild)	1 head of garlic, peeled, chopped
⅓ cup sugar	1 bunch cilantro, chopped

Editor's Tip

If you cut flowers from the garden (or get some from the florist), here's a tip on how to get them to last longer. Each day simply recut the stem, under warm water, up about a quarter of an inch. This will help the flowers keep absorbing water and stay fresher.

Combine all ingredients except cilantro. Bring to a boil; simmer about 1 hour. Add cilantro; cook another 10 minutes. Refrigerate or freeze salsa until ready to use.

Florence Simm
Auburn, WA

Yesterday's Paper Is Valuable

Here's how I make a new garden bed: Do not dig up sod or do anything like that to the area. In the fall, place 12 layers of newspaper over the area. (Do not use the colored, slick part—just the newsprint pages.) Cover the newspaper with at least 4 inches of good soil. Water it well, or let winter's snow and rain do the work. If you live in a dry, warm area, water regularly, and keep the area wet for 4 or 5 months. In the spring, your bed is ready for planting. Even if the paper does not completely decompose, it does keep the weeds down and it adds "good stuff" to the soil.

Ardith N. Morton
Merriman, NE

RECIPE: SUMMER SQUASH COMBO

5 yellow crookneck squash, cut into $\frac{1}{2}$-inch cubes

5 green calabacito squash, cut into $\frac{1}{2}$-inch cubes

2 green bell peppers, chopped

2 red bell peppers or pimiento, chopped

1 stick margarine

4 ears young sweet corn

Heat squash and peppers in a large skillet. Add margarine; stir until melted. Cover; cook on low until squash is almost entirely cooked. Cut corn from cob; stir into skillet mixture. Cover; cook on low about 10 minutes.

Options: Adding sausage will make this a complete meal. You can use all yellow squash if calabacito is not available.

Sharon L. Jones
Rye, CO

It All Blends in

I decided to get a new blender so I could use my dear old blender to blend my garbage and food scraps. It makes a wonderful, rich slurry that I take to my garden areas and just pour it into a hole I make with a trowel. I've got instant compost that works beautifully. No muss, no fuss, and no-wait composting!

During the winter the slurry can be frozen. You can thaw it in the spring or summer to add to your garden.

Betty Lou Kohl
Ogallala, NE

RECIPE: VEGETABLE STUFFED PEPPERS

3 green peppers

2 T. margarine

¼ cup chopped onion

1 cup fresh corn kernels

1 cup green beans, cooked

1 tomato, chopped

½ tsp. salt

Pepper to taste

½ cup grated cheddar cheese

Wash peppers; remove tops and seeds. Boil peppers in salted water for 5 minutes; drain. Sauté onions in margarine until onions are just soft. Mix corn, green beans, tomato, salt and pepper; add to onion mixture. Fill peppers with vegetable mixture; sprinkle cheese on top. Place stuffed peppers in baking dish and bake at 350°F for 25 minutes.

Options: You could add a few tablespoons of cooked rice or even some cubed cooked turkey or chicken.

Bonnie Warfel
Orange Park, FL

One Good Turn

If your containers only receive morning sun (or only afternoon sun), rotate them 180 degrees once a week to promote even growth. This is especially helpful when you have cascading flowers and greenery that tends to grow only in the direction of sunlight! If you have large, hard-to-handle containers, try using plant dollies underneath them.

Chandra R. White
Bremerton, WA

Editor's Tip

Mulching Materials

As you select mulching materials, consider where they will be used. Ornamental plantings look best when mulched with attractive materials such as chopped bark or pine needles. Vegetable gardeners often use newspaper or straw.

MATERIAL	PRIMARY BENEFIT	WHEN AND HOW TO APPLY
Lawn clippings	Builds soil structure. Moderates soil temperature. Conserves moisture.	Allow clippings to dry before applying. Apply a 1- to 4-inch layer that doesn't form a dense mat.
Chopped leaves	Suppresses weeds. Builds soil structure. Reduces soil temperature.	Chop or compost before using because whole leaves mat down. Mulch in winter or spring with a 3-inch layer.
Pine needles	Builds soil structure. Suppresses weeds. Good for acid-loving plants.	Apply a 2- to 4-inch layer around shrubs and trees. Pine needles tend to acidify the soil.
Bark nuggets	Conserves moisture. Suppresses weeds.	Apply a 2- to 3-inch layer around shrubs and trees, preferably over a roll-out mulch.
Straw or hay	Builds soil structure. Suppresses weeds. Moderates soil temperature. Conserves moisture.	Apply a 6-inch layer at planting time and as needed through the growing season. Straw usually contains fewer weed seeds than hay.

ROLL-OUT MULCHES

Paper, newspaper	Suppresses weeds. Conserves moisture.	Use between vining vegetables or in pathways between beds or rows. Cover with a thin layer of more attractive mulch. Turn under when partially decomposed.
Plastic weed barrier	Suppresses weeds. Conserves moisture.	Use beneath straw or grass clippings in places that are renovated at the end of the season. Reusable.
Plastic sheeting	Black plastic warms the soil and suppresses weeds. The light-reflective patterns that accompany red plastic mulch benefit tomatoes and some other crops, and deter nematodes.	Lay down plastic and anchor with rocks or soil at planting time. Can also be laid down to warm the soil so you can plant earlier in spring than you normally would. Use heavyweight reusable products.
Landscape fabric	Suppresses weeds. Long lasting.	Lay down at planting time and cut slits for plants. Can be difficult to cut and doesn't allow plants to spread beyond the cut hole.

Cool Plants

I use ice cubes to water plants (like spinach) to slow down the bolting. It works wonderfully, keeps the plants watered, and they last longer.

L. S. Kirkpatrick
Rio Rancho, NM

RECIPE: AVOCADO AND ROASTED CORN GUACAMOLE

1 cup fresh corn kernels

3 T. corn oil

2 large avocados, diced

1 large tomato, diced

¼ cup chopped cilantro, basil or parsley

2 T. minced onion

1 tsp. fresh jalapeño peppers

1 tsp. minced garlic

2 T. lime juice

1 tsp. vinegar

1½ tsp. salt

½ tsp. cumin

Heat oven to 450°F. Toss corn kernels with 1 tablespoon oil and place on a baking sheet. Roast, turning often, until golden (5 to 7 minutes); cool. Fold in avocado, tomato, cilantro, onion, jalapeño and garlic. Add lime juice, vinegar, salt, cumin and 2 tablespoons corn oil. Cover and refrigerate at least 3 to 4 hours. Serve with tortilla chips.

Serves 8.

Note: You can put all of the ingredients, except the avocado and tomatoes, together the day before.

Vi and John Howe
Miles City, MT

RECIPE:
TOMATO AND BASIL SANDWICH

2 slices Italian or French bread, toasted

1 slice Swiss cheese

Fresh basil leaves

Tomatoes, sliced

Balsamic vinaigrette

After toasting bread, place Swiss cheese on a bread slice. Spread basil over cheese; top with sliced tomatoes. Sprinkle balsamic vinaigrette over tomatoes and place remaining bread slice on top. Enjoy!

Merridy Kienitz
Blue Earth, MN

Editor's Tip

Run a simple test to see how your soil drains. Dig a hole 18 to 24 inches across and 18 to 24 inches deep. Fill the hole with water. If water disappears from the hole in 10 minutes or less you have sandy soil with fast drainage. If the water takes 1 hour or more to drain away you have clay soil or a hardpan (an impermeable layer of compacted soil beneath the soil surface) and the soil is poorly drained. There are many acceptable variations between these two extremes.

Darling Dahlias

When storing dahlias for the winter, make sure to put the stem end down. This allows any moisture to drain out and keeps the tubers from rotting. If you store the tubers in a very dry area, be sure to mist them several times through the dormant season to keep them from shriveling up and drying out. Also, when planting tall dahlias that need to be staked, put the stake in before planting to make sure you don't harm the tuber once it has started growing.

Donna Stewart
Kent, WA

Read All About It

I work full-time and have a family and home to care for, so my time and energy are limited. Plus, I don't own a tiller. So one day, as I pulled out my shovel to begin the chore of breaking and turning the soil, I came up with this idea. First, I laid out rocks, bricks and wood for borders. Then I placed several layers of newspaper (use only black and white pages, no colored ink) on the ground where I wanted to plant. (The newspapers don't allow sun to reach the grass and it dies.) On top of the papers I piled leaves and bark and a little sawdust. On top of that I layered potting soil.

For several weeks I planted bulbs and covered them with more leaves and sawdust. Now I have tulips, irises, crocuses, lilies, lily-of-the-valley, daffodils and many more varieties poking through the leaves—and no weeds!

Jennifer Mount
Via Email

RECIPE: FROZEN PICKLES

4 large cucumbers, sliced

3 yellow squash, sliced

3 large onions, sliced

1 large green pepper, sliced

2 cups sugar

1 cup vinegar

1 tsp. mustard seed

1 tsp. celery salt

Place cucumbers, squash, onions and green pepper in a large bowl. In a saucepan, boil sugar, vinegar, mustard seed and celery salt. Pour over vegetables. Cool; spoon into containers. Freeze.

Reta Dyson
Ozark, AL

RECIPE:
WINTER SQUASH WITH CHEESE AND THREE HERBS

2 lbs. butternut or buttercup squash

2 T. olive oil

$1\frac{1}{2}$ tsp. chopped, fresh thyme

2 T. fresh basil, chopped

1 tsp. fresh rosemary, chopped

$\frac{1}{2}$ cup grated mozzarella or Jack cheese

3 T. crumbled feta cheese

Preheat oven to 375°F.

Cut squash in half lengthwise; scoop out seeds and stringy fibers. Place squash, cut side down, in a small baking pan and add $\frac{1}{4}$ inch of water. Bake 45 minutes until flesh is tender. Remove from oven; drain. Cut into serving-size pieces; put into baking pan skin side down, flesh side up. Turn on broiler. Brush top and insides of squash pieces with olive oil, sprinkle with herbs and mozzarella cheese. Top with feta cheese. Place 3 to 4 inches from heat and broil until cheese is golden. Serve immediately.

Serves 6.

Mickie Reno
Gerber, CA

Editor's Tip

Compacted soil harms plants by making it harder for roots to penetrate, for water to permeate, and for oxygen to be available to plants. When you're working in your garden beds, avoid soil compaction by using a piece of plywood at least one foot square (larger is better) to place your weight on so you kneel or stand in one spot. This spreads out your weight.

RECIPE: ITALIAN VEGETABLE SOUP

1 lb. hamburger

1 cup onion, chopped

1 cup celery, chopped

1 cup carrots, diced

¼ tsp. garlic powder

1 qt. tomatoes

1 pint tomato sauce

15-oz. can kidney beans, undrained

1 pint canned corn

2 cups water

3 tsp. beef base

1 tsp. dried parsley

½ tsp. oregano

½ tsp. sweet basil

¼ tsp. pepper

2 cups shredded cabbage

1 pint green beans

½ cup small elbow macaroni

Brown hamburger with onion; drain grease. Add all other ingredients except cabbage, green beans and macaroni. Bring to a boil. Simmer, covered, on low heat, 20 minutes. Add cabbage, beans and macaroni. Boil, then simmer until ready to eat. You can add more spices if desired.

Jeannine Eisenbacher
Aurora, OR

The End Result Is Good

My family has raised several hundred rabbits commercially for over 30 years. Rabbit manure produces the very best fertilizer. I've used it with the traditional compost mixes, and it has made a great compost. However, rabbit manure is also a lazy gardener's fertilizer. Stack a pile of rabbit manure uncovered in the fall, turn it occasionally, and by spring you have a pile of organic powder that helps anything grow when you side-dress with it. Or even easier, just spread it on your garden in the spring before tilling.

G. L. Smith
Pea Ridge, AR

Haircut Appointment

'Autumn Joy' sedums often get top-heavy and flop over. As the flowers develop, they add weight and the whole plant sometimes falls down. To prevent this, cut 3 or 4 inches off the top of the plant in midsummer when it is about 18 inches tall. New stems will grow from the cut ends, and the plant will be more compact and sturdier—and flowering will be just as good in the fall.

Elizabeth Seibert
Katonah, NY

A Handy Clipper-Cleaner

I like to keep my hand clippers sterile. Constantly pulling out a large bottle of bleach or rubbing alcohol can be a pain, so I bought a 2-oz. plastic spray bottle and filled it with rubbing alcohol. I now just put it in my apron pocket with some paper towels and voilà—clean clippers.

If I've trimmed a plant that may have a fungus, etc., I can easily spray and wipe my clippers clean and move on to another plant. (You can find a 2-oz. spray bottle for about 69 cents in the cosmetics section of your pharmacy or dime store!)

Barbara Gibson
Seal Beach, CA

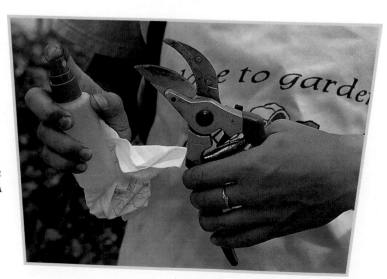

RECIPE: ZUCCHINI SQUARES (HORS D'OEUVRES)

1 cup biscuit mix

4 eggs, beaten

$\frac{1}{2}$ cup vegetable oil

$\frac{1}{2}$ cup grated Parmesan cheese

$\frac{1}{2}$ cup chopped onion

2 T. parsley

1 clove garlic, minced

$\frac{1}{2}$ tsp. seasoned salt

$\frac{1}{2}$ tsp. oregano

Dash of pepper

2 medium zucchini, thinly sliced

Combine all ingredients except zucchini; beat well. Stir in zucchini. Pour mixture into greased 13- x 9- x 2-inch baking pan. Bake at 350°F for 30 minutes or until golden brown. Let stand 10 minutes. Cut into squares.

Carol Burklin
Reidsville, NC

The Last Straw

The best way I have found to control weeds in my garden is a combination mulch of newspaper and straw. I water well, then lay newspaper between rows. I tear strips of paper to lay in between the plants. Then I cover it once with a layer of straw. It keeps weeds down, it works especially well for keeping sandy soil moist, and it keeps the water from splashing soil on the plants when I water. I used this for all my tomatoes and peppers with great success. (Most newspapers are now printed with soy-based ink, so the chemicals shouldn't be a problem.)

Cara McIlquham
Chippewa Falls, WI

RECIPE:
STUFFED PUMPKINS

4 mini pumpkins

2 cups cubed bread

1 cup diced onions

$\frac{1}{2}$ cup diced celery

1 tsp. dried marjoram

1 tsp. dried basil

$\frac{1}{2}$ tsp. dried oregano

1 tsp. olive oil

$\frac{1}{2}$ cup vegetable stock

Preheat oven to 325°F.

Cut off top of pumpkins; set aside. Scoop out seeds and membranes. Place pumpkin shells on baking sheet. In medium bowl, combine remaining ingredients. Pack stuffing tightly into pumpkin cavities. Cover with reserved tops. Bake until pumpkins are soft (about 45 minutes).

Janet Lowe
Tucson, AZ

Jeepers, Say the Creepers

For creeping ivy or creeping Charlie, mix $\frac{1}{4}$ cup Borax and 2 teaspoons Ivory dishwashing soap with a little hot water. Fill a gallon jug with the mix and cold water. Put it into spray bottle and spray your weeds.

Ethel Griffin
Via Email

Liquid Gold

If you have an aquarium, each time you change the water, feed it to your houseplants. It works similar to fish-emulsion fertilizers and it doesn't smell. The plants love it.

Elaine Mull
Jacksonville, FL

Hammering That Mildew

I had a problem with powdery mildew on several of my plants until I finally found a natural control. Add one teaspoon of baking soda diluted with 32 ounces of water in a spray bottle. After mixing the baking soda and water, add one teaspoon of dish soap (this helps the mixture stick) and shake it well.

Susan Hilbert
Reno, NV

RECIPE:
CAJUN POTATO SALAD

4 large red potatoes

4 eggs

2 T. yellow mustard

1½ cups mayonnaise

1 medium bell pepper, chopped

1 large dill pickle, chopped

2 stalks celery, chopped

8 green onions, chopped

½ cup chopped parsley

½ cup sweet pickle relish

1 tsp. salt

1 tsp. red cayenne pepper

2 tsp. black pepper

1 tsp. white pepper

4-5 drops Tabasco sauce

Bring a large pot of water to a boil. Add potatoes and eggs; return to simmer and cook 15 minutes. Remove eggs; dip in cold water. Continue to cook potatoes until tender. Drain and cool. When cool, peel potatoes and cut into cubes. Peel eggs and chop. Combine eggs with all the rest of the ingredients. Mix well. Pour over potatoes and toss to coat.

NOTE: This is very spicy. Cut down on the pepper for a milder taste.

Leon Arnold
Brevard, NC

Bottle Up the Weeds

To kill weeds with RoundUp or other herbicides and not spray "good plants" growing near the weeds, cut the bottom out of a gallon milk jug or plastic juice or pop bottle. Then cut the top down to the handle.

Turn it upside down over the weed and spray the herbicide into the bottle or jug. This way you won't spray more than the plant you are aiming at. If a smaller area is affected, use a smaller plastic bottle.

Ethel Griffin
Via Email

The Desert Difference

Here's what I've learned after years of desert gardening:

- **Treat a new plant as being one shade shadier than normal. For example, full-sun plants go in partial shade. This is especially true for perennials in their first summer.**

- **You can grow wrong-zone plants if you stick to this rule: If it's meant for a colder zone, bring it inside in the summer. If it's for a warmer zone, bring it inside in the winter.**

Erin Lale
Las Vegas, NV

Boxing in the Bed

We made a new shrub bed in our lawn and didn't spray or dig out any grass beforehand. We laid down a layer of cardboard boxes and thick layers of newspaper, then put a thick layer of bark mulch over the top. It worked wonderfully!

Valerie Giesbrecht
Othello, WA

RECIPE: MARINATED ORANGE SALMON FILLETS

$\frac{1}{2}$ cup orange juice

$\frac{1}{2}$ cup soy sauce

2 T. chopped parsley

3 T. olive oil

2 small cloves garlic

1 tsp. crushed, dried basil or 1 T. finely chopped fresh basil

2 to 3 salmon fillets

Combine all ingredients, except the salmon, in a baking dish. Remove skin from salmon fillets and refrigerate in marinade for approximately 4 to 6 hours. Turn fillets often.

To cook, place fish on hot barbecue grill or put salmon in grill basket before placing on grill. Baste often with remaining marinade until salmon flakes with a fork, approximately 20 to 30 minutes.

Serves 6 to 10.

Bonnie Childs
Skwentina, AK

A Spicy Solution

When I have an unhealthy-looking rose bush, I plant garlic chives around it. Somehow in a short time the rose really perks up.

Norma Musser
Womelsdorf, PA

RECIPE: TAMARI CHICKEN

4 chicken breasts, pounded flat

Tamari sauce

6 to 8 chard leaves, steamed

1 green onion, chopped

2 T. chopped lemon basil

1/2 tsp. Greek seasoning

1/4 to 1/3 cup Parmesan cheese

Sesame seeds

Sprinkle chicken with tamari sauce; let them sit while you prepare other ingredients. Lay 1 to 2 chard leaves on each breast. Sprinkle with onion, basil, Greek seasoning and cheese. Roll up chicken. Place in a small, oiled baking dish; sprinkle with sesame seeds. Bake at 350°F for approximately 20 minutes.

Alice Ruleman
Memphis, TN

Grounds for Success

One gardening trick that works for me is to feed all the acid-loving plants (such as dogwoods, azaleas, roses, hollies, spruces, magnolias and nandinas) used coffee grounds, tea leaves and leftover coffee and tea. I bring home coffee grounds and tea leaves from the local Lions Club pancake breakfast or a big church dinner. It's much better than tossing them in the garbage.

Jean H. Goddard
Bowling Green, KY

Be a Fall Guy

We like to transplant in the fall when the plant's root system is still healthy, but heading towards a state of dormancy. Always put compost in the hole of a new transplant to ensure plenty of nutrition when the plant "wakes up" in early spring. If transplanting can be done on a rainy day, that's even better—you won't have to water afterward. The transplant will receive a natural watering.

Peggy R. Raposa
Coventry, RI

Deep Thoughts on Tomatoes

When transplanting tomatoes, take off the bottom leaves and set the plant extra deep. Tomatoes will put out more roots from the buried stem and produce a stronger, healthier plant.

Betty J. Burke
Odessa, TX

We're Rooting for You

If you are rooting cuttings in water, change the water every day. Fresh water has more oxygen than stagnant water, and your cuttings will root faster and have stronger roots. If you have a lot of cuttings to root in water, get a small water pump like the ones used in fish tanks.

Alice Gibbons
Las Vegas, NV

Pooling Resources

We pumped the rainwater off our pool cover in late winter and early spring into two large barrels so we have rain water to water plants and flowers. They have lids so they don't evaporate either.

David Hutchison
Monticello, KY

RECIPE: QUICK KALITSOUNIA

1 egg, beaten

4 oz. feta cheese, crumbled

1 T. parsley

1 tube refrigerated buttermilk biscuits

Sesame seeds (optional)

Combine egg, feta cheese and parsley. Separate biscuits. On lightly floured surface, roll each biscuit to a 4-inch circle about $\frac{1}{8}$ inch thick. Place 1 tablespoon of cheese mixture in center of each dough circle. Fold opposite edges of circle to center. Fold remaining two opposite edges to center forming a square packet. Pinch edges to seal. Place rolls seam side up on a greased baking sheet. Brush the tops with beaten egg. Sprinkle with sesame seeds if desired. Bake at 425°F for 10 to 12 minutes. Serve hot.

Rosemary Sanders
Follansbee, WV

A Good Garden "Hose"

I transplant my tomato seedlings into half-gallon milk cartons with the bottoms cut out. I place a strip of panty hose, knotted and stretched, over the bottom and sides of the carton. To plant the seedlings outdoors in mid-April (about a month before the safe frost date), I surround them with jugs of water and then wrap with bubble wrap fastened with clothespins. When the weather warms, I gradually open and remove the plastic wrap.

Ruth I. Morton
Rochester, NY

Join the Booster Club

Here's what I call the morning boost: I save up eggshells and coffee grounds, mix them in a blender with enough water to cover, then pour the mixture onto the soil around plants. This booster mix serves many purposes:

- The liquid serves as a fertilizer.
- The mulch from the grounds and shells deters slugs and snails.
- Deer can't stand the egg smell and stay out of the garden.
- In the spring I dig the "mulch" into the soil and start the process over again, adding organic matter to the soil.

Christine M. Doyle
Waterford, ME

Garden
Solutions

A gardener telling you that he or she never
has gardening problems to solve, or
challenges to tackle, is a gardener not quite
telling the truth.

Here are members' best ideas for solving the
gardening challenges that are always
presenting themselves and making our
gardening life interesting.

Making Your Bed

Here's how to create a garden bed in one day:

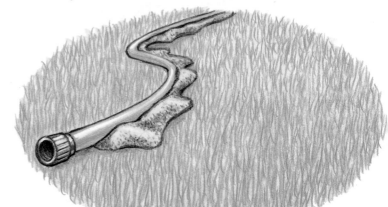

1. Use a garden hose to shape the bed, and then make a line with sand beside the hose so that you can move the hose when you dig. An edger makes a neat first cut.

2. With a spade, remove 6 to 12 inches of the grass along the whole border and slope the edge.

3. Mow the new bed on your lowest mower setting. Rake up any piles and put them in your compost bin.

4. Lay down landscape fabric 3 inches from the edge, overlapping each piece 3 inches, and pin it in place with stakes.

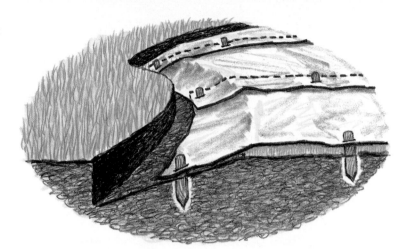

5. Cover the bed with 2 or 3 inches of shredded mulch.

6. To place a plant, push mulch aside, cut an "x" in the fabric, remove the grass from the section, and set the plant inside. Replace the fabric and mulch. Water well.

You'll save a lot of work, and have a weed-free, beautiful bed this way.

Vicki L. Guliano
Port St. Lucie, FL

Editor's Tip

Here's a trick they use in the vineyards, so if you grow grapes yourself, you might try it. Winemakers plant roses at the end of each row of grapes. Roses—especially Hybrid Teas—are more susceptible to many diseases than the grapes are. When mildew and other maladies show up on the roses, the grape growers know that it will threaten the grapes shortly. The growers then know it's time to take immediate and appropriate action.

A Tired New Idea

This is what my husband does for the tomato and squash plants in our Zone 3 gardens: He put tires around the tomato plants. Then he puts water in the tires about every 3 or 4 mornings. It takes the water all day to heat up from the sun, so it's warm inside the tires when we cover them with plastic at night. As a result our plants grow and ripen faster. It also helps keep the tomatoes up off the ground.

Mrs. Ralph R. Traughber
Swan Valley, ID

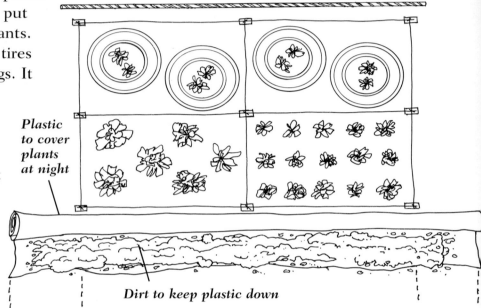

Plastic to cover plants at night

Dirt to keep plastic down

Clothespins to the Rescue

When frost threatens, grab your row covers or blankets and a handful of spring-clip clothespins. Put the covers over your tomato cages and use the clothespins to hold them in place. It's effective and much quicker than tying the row covers to the tomato cages.

Nancy Stoddard
Sault Ste. Marie, MI

Hand-Water Helper

Last summer, with the drought on, we had to water the gardens each day with a sprinkling can we filled with 5-gallon buckets. Because the hole in the sprinkling can was too small to pour into, and the 5-gallon bucket is heavy when full, I invented this helper. Take a 1-gallon milk jug with no lid. Cut an oval hole above the shoulder and right in front. It fills quickly in the bucket, and pours perfectly into the small hole of the sprinkling can.

Janet Park
Oakland, MD

A Homemade Sun-Beater

If the only place you have to install a pond, bed or sitting area gets too much sun you can build a trellis out of 2 by 4s. For example, I made a trellis 7 feet tall by 8 feet long by 2 feet deep. I covered the ends with one layer of pre-made lattice and I used two layers on the top for more sun screening. I placed it so that it casts shadow over my 125-gallon pond as the sun moves across my backyard.

I planted clematis at both ends of the trellis to give me even more shade in future years. I considered it a success because algae did not choke my pond this summer. Some algae growth is normal and unavoidable, but other water plants also help by competing with the oxygen the algae need.

Douglas Taylor
Decatur, IL

Handy When It's Hot

When working in my Central Florida yard, I can get mighty hot. I make sure I drink plenty of water or sports drinks while mowing the grass. To make access to water more convenient, I bought a bicycling water bottle and holder. Then I mounted it to the handle of my mower with two O-clamps. Now, my water is within easy reach and I can get the job finished much more quickly. (Putting the bottle in the freezer for about 30 minutes before starting keeps it nice and cold.)

Jeffrey Estep
Chelsea, AL

Kitchen-Drawer Weeders

An old fork and cheap paring knife are some of my best tools for slicing off weeds just below the surface. They are small enough to reach into tight places that other tools can't reach.

Gay Swecker
Motley, MN

A Greenhouse on a Stick

I grow lots of vegetables and tender annuals that need protection from late-spring cold spells, so I came up with this handy milk-jug storage and carrier device: Plastic milk jugs with the bottoms cut off make great mini-greenhouses. To store them when the weather warms up, I take an old mop handle and push a nail through the hanging hole at one end of the handle. Next I slide the cut milk jugs on it, fitting one over the other. I store them neatly in my garden shed over winter, and in the spring, I just pick up the stack by the pole and head for the garden. I just slide a jug off as I need it and the others stay together instead of blowing around the garden.

Harriet Link
Renville, MN

A Trickle Trick

Put one tiny pinhole in a gallon jug to slowly water a plant without runoff. (It may take a few hours.) I used this when I lived in Arizona for beautiful tomatoes!

Gay Swecker
Motley, MN

As Right as Rain

I use a couple of old plastic barrels with lids to collect rainwater from my downspouts. I take off the lid when rain is in the forecast, then add an ounce or two of bleach when I put the lid back on, to keep the water fresh. I use collected rainwater to keep my compost moist and water my veggie garden too. The bleach dissipates rather quickly so it's safe to use anywhere in the garden.

(Editor's Note: Keep the lids on when it's not raining, to prevent mosquitoes from laying eggs in the water.)

Catherine Stepalavich
Middletown, RI

Rainwater Through the Hose

Keep a rain barrel as near to the garden as possible. There is nothing that compares to water from the sky, and the plants know it. Water the plants from the bottom of the barrel by using this trick: Place the end of a long hose into the rain barrel. One end of the hose should be completely submerged and secured. Apply suction to the other end of the hose. It will cause the water in the barrel to keep moving through the hose by inertia (that is, a body in motion will stay in motion). It helps if the level of the water is above the level of the area to be watered. Use a regular hose or a soaker hose with holes in it that is placed strategically along the garden floor. You won't have to move it every time you water the garden. When watering is completed, simply stop the flow by removing the submerged end of the hose.

Peggy R. Raposa
Coventry, RI

Editor's Tip

The clear plastic bags that you get from the dry cleaner can be recycled into mini-greenhouses. Make a cylinder of chicken wire big enough to cover your plant to be protected, but still leaving enough space for more growth. Cover the sides of the chicken wire with the bags and tie them on. As days get warmer, remove the greenhouses and replace them about an hour before sunset. If the weather gets really cold, invert a cardboard carton over the greenhouse.

Greener Pastures

Having trouble growing grass on a sloped location?
Here are some "sod-making" tips:

- **Grow grass on cookie sheets or small boxes. When it's established, gently lift a whole sheet of grass—just loosen the soil before placing it down on the slope. Then put the grass in place, water gently and regularly. You'll soon see the new grass growing there.**

- **You can also loosen the soil of the slope and add deep plugs of grass from other locations in the yard. Water them regularly.**

Donna King
Lake Butler, FL

That's a Wrap

If your tomato cages are made of heavy reinforcement wire, you can extend the growing season by simply wrapping heavy plastic sheets around them.

Irmgard Haskins
Garberville, CA

A Quick Fix

One morning we saw that the birdbath was knocked over. The basin was all right, but the base was broken beyond repair. (We think that maybe a raccoon knocked it over.) I wanted it fixed right away—so I used two large terra-cotta flowerpots butted end to end and held in place with a nut, bolt and two rubber washers. It's working out just fine and saved a lot of time, shopping and money!

Joanne Drake
St. Petersburg, FL

Bottled Wisdom

Here's how to protect tomatoes and other tender plants from frost: Place six or seven plastic liter bottles in a circle. Secure them with duct tape. Place them around tender plants in the early spring. Fill them with water and secure the lid. The bottles will absorb heat from the sun and release it slowly at night, protecting your plants.

Ruth E. Anderson
Tooele, UT

Coffee Keeps 'em Warm

I use 39-ounce coffee cans with the top and bottom taken off. Then I put the clean plastic lids back on them and put them over my cabbage, broccoli, cauliflower and kohlrabi. The plants can be put out as much as 3 weeks earlier this way. This also recycles the cans.

Lloyd Bahr
Camas, WA

The Rewards
of Recycling

Conserving resources—such as soil, water, materials and your own money—is always a worthwhile endeavor.

Here are the ways members told us they do recycling: re-using and rejuvenating old things in their gardens. These are ideas you'll want to use too.

A Swingin' Time in the Greenhouse

Here's how you can make an inexpensive greenhouse by using an old swing set. (You can find these swings at garage sales for giveaway prices).

Remove the swings and wrap the frame with 6-mil clear plastic. To hold the clear plastic in place make clamps from 4-inch lengths of plastic pipe, and put dirt around the bottom edges of the frame to keep out the cold air. You can install a zippered door by cutting one from a tent. (These doors can also be found at garage sales.)

Mary C. Nichols
Arlington, VA

Office Composting

I add the shredded paper from my paper shredder to the compost bin. It is a great source of "brown" material because it mixes in easily and decomposes quickly. (If a lot of "brown" is needed, you can shred strips of newspaper.)

For a source of "green" material, I periodically collect coffee grounds from my local coffeehouse or restaurant.

Loretta Fisher
Anacortes, WA

The News from "Compostville"

I have used old newspapers in my garden for more than 20 years. In the beginning, I just put newspapers between rows of vegetables and covered them with grass clippings or straw. Since I used hilled-up rows, it was easy to till the raised rows in the fall and cover the newspapers and clippings so they would decay over the winter. This worked fine for several years, but the drawback was that I had more newspapers than I knew what to do with.

Then I discovered that I could use my chipper/shredder to chop up the newspapers and use them as mulch. The shredder does not do a good job with dry newspapers, so I soak them in water for a few hours. The wet newspapers shred up into a mush that can either be added immediately to a compost pile or set aside to dry out and used as mulch around vegetables and flowers. I have done this for 13 years and can't count the tons of newspapers I have recycled into the soil. My raised bed gardens now contain beautiful black composted soil that was nothing more than hard clay in the beginning. (I use a Troy-Bilt 5-horsepower shredder, and I remove the discharge screen so the newspapers won't clog. The blades alone do the job well.)

Wayne Hamburger
Eldorado, IL

A $7.00 Compost Bin

I bought a plastic garbage can on wheels with a locking lid. Then I drilled quarter-size holes all over, including the lid and bottom. I then filled the can with all those wonderful yard and kitchen scraps. I turned the mixture with a shovel  whenever I made a deposit, and by the end of summer and winter I had 30 gallons of wonderful compost. And the worms are plentiful!

Nan Binkley
Bartlett, TN

Readable Mulch

If you don't like to weed, but don't like the look or cost of black plastic or mulch, use newspaper. Last summer all I had to do was put between 5 and 10 layers of non-laminated newspaper under a thin layer of mulch. In the fall I used a broom to sweep up the extra mulch. I managed to save nearly half the mulch, which I stored in large buckets. Not only did I save time on weeding, but quite a bit of money too. By the end of the summer nearly all the paper had biodegraded so it was no trouble turning it into the soil.

Teresa Cea
Clintondale, NY

From Laundry to Garden

I don't throw away the cotton lint from my dryer. Instead I use it in my compost pile. It keeps the pile loose and it doesn't get compacted.

Also, in spring I put lint out in my yard. The birds love to gather it, along with twigs and such, to build their nests. They line their nests with the lint to make it warm and cozy for their little ones.

Christine L. Riddle
Sacramento, CA

Shake a Leg!

Use old nylon stockings or a leg cut off old pantyhose for dusting garden plants. Put the dust, wood ash, or whatever you use in the stocking. Grasp each end of the stocking and gently shake over and around your garden plants.

Martha J. Kehr
East Otto, NY

Jug-Ling in the Garden

Fill milk jugs with water and place them directly behind your plants (on the north side). This will help block the wind, plus the water will be warmed by the sun and will radiate heat for the plants after sundown. Many plants, such as tomatoes and peppers, benefit from this additional heat.

Another tip for milk jugs: Cut up old jugs into plant tags. Print plant names on them with a waterproof marker and stick them next to your plants for an inexpensive identification system. Then you'll know at a glance which plant you are looking at.

Nancy Stoddard
Sault Ste. Marie, MI

Pooling Your Resources

You can make a free, very useful garden tool from a recycled plastic swimming pool. These are usually thrown on the trash at the end of summer when they have developed holes. No problem! The small leaks are needed for your new leaf container, or onion/potato/canna bulb-washing tub. Simply punch a couple of holes below the "lip"of the pool; thread a sturdy rope through the holes, and tie the two ends in a knot, leaving enough rope between the pool and you for a comfortable lead rope. For storage, simply hang the pool on the garage wall by the rope.

Here are some uses for your recycled swimming pool:
- Dump in bushels of leaves and drag them to your compost pile.
- Wash off vegetables, plants pots, etc., and have the dirt filter out the bottom.
- Use the pool to corral pots of plants that are being hardened off in the spring—even cover them with another pool at night or when it rains.
- Deposit and hand gather piles of weeds or prunings.

Ruth Meszaros
Ladysmith, WI

Two-Ring Ceremony

I have found an effective way to water a new plant without watering other established plants. Cut the bottom out of a 5-gallon plastic pail and then cut the pail in half to make two rings. Place one of the plastic rings about an inch deep around the new plant. Water with a sprinkling can to moisten the soil enough so you can push the rim of the plastic pail about one inch into the soil. Then water your plant. The plastic ring will hold in the water and allow it to seep slowly around the roots of your new plant. I use this method when I set out new daylilies and it works great.

I also use these same plastic rings to hold pine needle mulch around daylilies which I plant in the fall. Otherwise, the wind will blow the mulch away.

Susan Huwaldt
Neligh, NE

Blocky but Beautiful

Here's my portable planting border:

First, spray-paint cement blocks to blend with or accent your yard.
Then plant the "cavities" with annuals that won't get very tall, such
as marigolds or alyssum. In the fall, the blocks can be moved to
allow for winter snow removal.

Janice Kessler
Sault Ste. Marie, MI

A Lot at Stake

While looking for something to use as a temporary shade for a transplant that needed protection from the hot sun, I ran across an old discarded umbrella. I attached the umbrella shank to a garden stake with a couple of hose clamps. I use the staked umbrella by pushing it into the ground to provide temporary shade for any new plant or transplants. It can be stored easily with other garden equipment: Just loosen the hose clamps, remove the garden stake and close the umbrella.

However, my umbrella is seldom in storage. When the rains started last fall, the umbrella was a great solution for keeping birdseed (and birds) dry in a low ground-level feeder.

Lucille Cassel
Eugene, OR

Shred It and Reap

When this past growing season ended, I was not able to find enough mulch for my huge expanded garden area, especially for my strawberries and other berries. Because I always try to recycle, I put my old letters through the paper shredder, and I also shredded old newspaper to use for mulch. In the spring I will remove this paper mulch and compost it. I have used this in the past to my satisfaction. It also makes the cost of gardening a little less expensive for someone on a tight budget.

Steven Lee Wortman
Rhinelander, WI

Taking A-Fence at Compost

My husband took down part of our crumbling 5-foot-high picket fence when it was about to fall down. He took the old pickets off half of the fencing and filled in

the empty spaces on the rest of the fencing with them. He then cut them into 8-foot sections, which he fastened into a square. He cut the front side down to about 3 feet high and the other sides to 4 feet high. This is now our compost bin. He plans to add another bin when he takes down the remainder of the fence. This is recycling at its best!

Maureen D. Goodwin
Framingham, MA

A Wire-Service Story

I recycle inexpensive wire flowerbed borders. I use them to anchor the plastic mulch in my raised vegetable beds. I've discovered many advantages of the wire border over standard wire anchors:

- Rather than anchor a few inches at a time, you can anchor a foot or more depending on whether you take the segments apart or leave them intact.

- They provide boundaries and lend organization to the garden.

- They are easy to locate when you decide to take up the plastic mulch.

- The size makes them easy to locate and hard to lose after being stored away for the winter.

- At approximately $3.00 for 10 feet, it's very inexpensive. When taken apart and spaced at intervals, it's even more economical!

Karen Daniel
Atlanta, TX

A Flat-Out Better Way

If you ask the people at the supermarket fish department for fish containers, they often will give you Styrofoam containers that are ideal for flats. You can poke drainage holes in the bottom. If you have been using grape crates as flats, these Styrofoam containers are lighter, a bit smaller, easier to handle and will not rot.

Mary Anne McMurray
Monmouth Beach, NJ

Using Paper to the Max

Buy a paper shredder at an office supply store. Do not buy the cheapest one, but invest in the store's additional warranty for a few extra dollars. Then shred all of your newspaper (except glossy print) and mix it with water. Use it in compost piles or as mulch around plants. You can even use a shredder that makes confetti and mix the confetti with grass seed to re-seed slopes and hills. That way the seed stays put until it sprouts.

Michael Courtright
Oklahoma City, OK

Free Rain Barrels

We found that we could get industrial-size drums free from a local company. After scrubbing them out, we sliced off the tops to make a replaceable lid. We connected them tandem-style with short pipe and washers. Then we rigged up long gardening hoses to submersible sump pumps, which gave a gentle stream. Now we don't have to lug sprinkling cans or buckets all around. It saves the back and we can move the pump from barrel to barrel as the need arises.

Patty Roosa
Ravenna, OH

Bucket Brigade

I've found I can use my old plastic pails for watering. I just poke a small hole near the bottom of 5-gallon pails, fill them with water and place them next to young trees which need extra water when getting established.

Susan Huwaldt
Neligh, NE

135

Hanging on
Every Word

Here are several ways I use old wire coat hangers:

- Pull them into a diamond shape, straighten the "hook" and turn to
  the inside to hold oranges for orioles, and other fruits (like apples)
  for birds. You can hang these from a tree branch.

- Pull them out and use them to hang hummingbird feeders in the
  shade (for instance, under tree branches) so the sun won't cause the
  liquid to expand and leak.

- You can also use old coat hangers to hang tender house plants
  outside in the summer.

Janice E. Kessler
Sault Ste. Marie, MI

A-Peel-Ing to the Kids

I am a teacher and many of my students bring bananas for snacks. I have a "recycling" can for the peels. I've explained composting and recycling to my students. They know that every other month I bury a whole banana peel by each of my roses to feed them. My roses are beautiful and often we have enough peels for students to take home to bury by their roses. Even the parents are learning to recycle!

Susan Corso
Lancaster, CA

Fab Frost-Protectors

Fabric stores sell polyester quilt batting on large rolls (45 or 54 inches wide). These are 30 feet long, lightweight and easy to cut with scissors. They can be used as a row cover and then rolled up again to store in a large garbage bag. We have also used it on the seedlings in the greenhouse when there was a frosty forecast and it saved peppers and tomatoes.

Janice E. Kessler
Sault Ste. Marie, MI

Regular Brushing Means Clean Tools

Can the lowly toilet bowl brush be a useful garden tool? Well, maybe not in the garden, but I find it very useful after gardening. With its 16-inch slightly angled handle, round head and bristles with just the right degree of stiffness, I find that it makes a great cleaning brush for all of those messy and muddy gardening tools. I use this brush, along with a hose and spray nozzle, to clean everything from a garden trowel to a lawn mower. It even works well, along with the hose, to scrub out the grass clippings that collect under the deck of my lawn mower.

Lucille Cassel
Eugene, OR

Editor's Tip

If you have a cut Christmas tree, don't just toss it or burn it after the holidays. Use it to feed the birds in winter. Set your tree outside with suet cakes, birdfeeders, cut oranges, apple slices or other treats. Be sure to place it where you'll enjoy seeing the show as much as the birds will enjoy the food.

In the spring, cut up the boughs and use them as mulch under plants that like acidic soil—azaleas, rhododendrons or roses, for example.

A Block-and-Board Bench

I made a bench with decorative ends and placed it between my lilac bushes. I made it by recycling two concrete blocks. On each block I placed a seat made of a sturdy recycled flat board. I planted vinca and English ivy under the bench and around the ends of the block. Then I painted the blocks with plain yogurt and buttermilk which forms a crust-like, scaly greenish moss. My bench area is very pretty, and I sit there and dream how my new garden will look in full bloom.

Mary Ann Marino
West Pittsburgh, PA

Melons on a Tray

To keep melons from insect damage and rot, cut gallon jugs in half lengthwise and burn drainage holes in the sides and bottoms with a soldering iron. Place the jug halves under melons while they're small. To store the jugs when not in use, run a string through the holes and hang them. This works great and I have used these jug-trays for years.

Kenneth Fulk
Albion, IN

Raking It in

Here's my easy "rake tool holder": Simply hang the head of the rake upside down in a convenient place, and hang small garden tools between the tines.

Marge Steinberger
Howell, MI

Rewired and Ready

Everybody has ratty and bent wire hangers in their closets that they just can't seem to throw away. Well, you can recycle them for use in the garden. Use wire cutters to cut off the top and two corners (leave about 3 inches on each side) and now you have arched stakes to hold down landscape fabric. Or, you can do as I did last season—stake soaker hose in a snakelike pattern through my veggie beds. The straight lengths that are left between the corners that were cut off can be used as stakes secured with bread ties beside tall plants.

Joanne Collins
Nashua, NH

A New Soccer Fan

Gardening has me down on my knees continually but I can't take much kneeling. I once tried leftover football or wrestling knee pads, but they fell apart. Then I found soccer knee pads at a garage sale. They're much heavier and get the job done easily.

Madelyn M. Wise
Decorah, IA

Bits 'n' Pieces

Sometimes you just can't classify an idea, other than to say, "That is a great tip and it needs to be told to the world!"

Here are those bits and pieces of members' gardening lore—smart ideas to help you smoothly travel your road to practical gardening success.

Kneeling with Ease

Take a pair of old pants and cut rectangles of scrap fabric from them large enough to cover the knee and shin area of your favorite gardening pants. Then iron on fabric-bonding tape to the back side of the fabric—the bottom and sides. Apply tape only on three edges, then iron on to the front knee area of the pants. (Make sure the open end will be on top of each knee.) Then slide a piece of foam rubber into this "pocket" and save your knees the pain of kneeling on hard ground!

Shirley Wilcox
Nichols, NY

What a Vine Idea!

Making grapevine wreaths can be difficult without an extra pair of hands. An easy way to keep the size and shape is to use dowels as the outer brace. Just stick them into the ground in a circle. Then wrap the vines inside the circle of dowels. The shape is contained by the outside edge dowels. The dowels can be easily reused to make any size wreath.

Karen J. Pawlovich
Haslett, MI

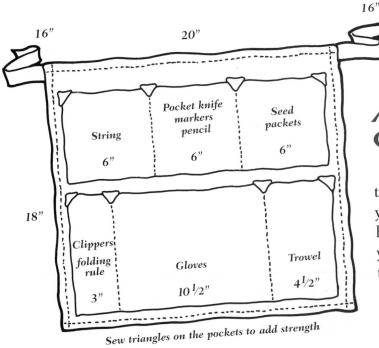

Sew triangles on the pockets to add strength

All-Purpose Garden Garb

A garden apron is the handiest thing and you can easily make one yourself with this diagram. Use heavy cloth and you will find yourself putting on this apron every time you head for the garden.

Mitzi Earl
Salem, AR

Handling a Tool Problem

Spray tool handles with a brightly colored paint so that they are easier to find if left somewhere. They are also easy to identify if a friend has "forgotten" to return a tool borrowed from you.

Karen J. Pawlovich
Haslett, MI

Pickle Those Weeds

I kill weeds that grow in cracks of sidewalks by pouring full-strength white vinegar on the weeds. The high acidity in the vinegar will kill the weeds almost instantly.

Mary Ann Marino
West Pittsburgh, PA

Tote Your Tools

Do you have worn out screwdrivers, pliers and tweezers in your toolbox? Don't toss them out—toss them into your garden tool tote. The screwdriver is great for prying up small stones, bricks and the like when they are in the way. The pliers are great for getting a grip on and moving things you don't want to touch—like poison oak or prickly weeds. The tweezers are for getting stickers out of yourself or your gloves.

D. Terry
Steele, AL

Editor's Tip

If an old paring knife has lost its usefulness in the kitchen, add it to your gardening tool kit. Its small, pointed blade makes it a terrific tool for cutting fibrous roots or weeds growing in cracks.

Quick 'n' Easy Steppingstones

Instead of building molds, pouring concrete, curing the concrete, digging holes to match the shape and depth of the steppingstones, hauling stones to where they're going, adding proper depth of sand base, leveling the stones in place and filling in around each stone—whew! Try this:

1. **Dig a 4-inch-deep hole, the shape of the desired steppingstone—where you want the stone.**

2. **Add an inch or so of sand.**

3. **Lay scraps of chicken wire or any odd wire (slightly bent) on sand to reinforce.**

4. **Pour concrete in place.**

5. **Keep moist until cured.**

Tip: Stones seem less likely to crack during the winter if the bottom of the stone is irregularly shaped.

Mrs. Teri Caddle
Clayton, IL

Giving Mud the Boot

I want to share a little tip I discovered by experimenting. I purchased a pair of boots to wear while working in the garden. However, the soles have deep ridges which fill up with mud. I remembered how a non-stick spray keeps food from sticking to my pans, so I tried it on the sole of my boots and, surprisingly, it worked! The mud stayed off.

Ann Licht
Dearborn Heights, MI

Editor's Tip

If you have occasional use for a heavy-duty chipper or shredder but don't want to rent or buy one by yourself, see about sharing one with your neighbors. If a few other people share the cost, it's not such a big bite out of the pocketbook. Everyone gets to use it when they need to, and it's nearby when you need it. This is a good idea for a tiller or any larger-ticket tool if everyone understands the ground rules.

Gardening with a Camera

Here are four ways a camera can help you grow a better garden *and* enjoy it even more:

- I create invitations using blank note cards with favorite garden photos glued to the front. These can be mailed to friends, inviting them to a personalized garden tour. (You can also use 4 x 6 photos as postcards.)

- Photos provide great documentation of what is planted in each garden area. I have several islands and borders, so I photograph each area in the spring, summer and fall (and sometimes in winter). I file these with my site maps, creating a fairly good planting record. I find this especially helpful for keeping track of spring bulbs.

- Photos provide an excellent history of individual trees and shrubs. For example, it's interesting to look back after 20 or 30 years and marvel at the little twig that is now a towering tree.

- Plant a tree the year your child is born. Then start a tradition of photographing the child by the tree on his/her birthday or on the first day of school each year. It's fun to see the changes in each!

Shirley Polen
Durand, MI

Timely Twine

For the many tying-up jobs around the house and garden, buy baler twine in bulk at the local farm supply store or co-op. Place the roll into a 5-gallon plastic pail, drill a hole in the lid, and carry it to wherever needed.

Delbert Nichols
Springfield, OH

Editor's Tip

If you need the strength of twine but don't like the look or thickness, try fishing line. If you don't fish, try getting some for free from sporting goods stores—they often collect old line for recycling. Fishing line is good for stringing overhead party lights, too.

Drips for Trips

Punch several pinholes in a plastic gallon jug, set it in the ground next to a plant that is not yet established, fill it with water and recap it. This will supply water for your plant for a few days while you're away.

Diana Smith
Kelso, WA

"101" Uses for Bleach Jugs

Making a plant saucer from the bottom of a plastic bleach jug is a good idea, but don't throw away the rest of the jug. The top makes a useful funnel and the midsection provides a multitude of labels. A sharp utility knife cuts the plastic easily.

Cut out the midsection and slice down one side of the cylinder you've made so that you can flatten it out. Then cut this into strips of whatever width you want and cut the strips into equal parts.

As for the top, it makes a perfect "hot cap" for plants that go out in the garden. When you plant tomatoes, eggplant or peppers in the garden, set the plastic hot cap over them to protect against a late-season chill.

Bonnie Warfel
Orange Park, FL

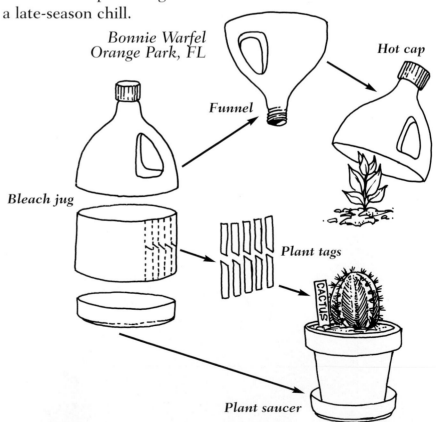

Bleach jug

Funnel

Hot cap

Plant tags

Plant saucer

Editor's Tip

When removing large tree branches, make three cuts to keep the limb from splintering and injuring the trunk:

1. Make the first cut 12 to 24 inches from the branch attachment, sawing until the blade begins to stick or bind: This takes pressure off the branch, preventing binding, for the next cuts.

2. Make the second cut on top of the branch 1 inch out from the first cut.

3. Remove the stub with your third cut, sawing it off just above the branch collar.

A Cheap Cleaning Tool

Use the inexpensive flat wooden or plastic kitchen tool called a "pot scraper" to clean mud and dirt off your hand tools, boots and shovels.

Esther Marshall
Opelika, AL

No-Mess Mesh

Use those plastic mesh strawberry baskets—upside down—in a bowl or vase to hold your cut-flower arrangement in place.

Leavette Galloway
Douglasville, GA

Quick 'n' Clean

Put leftover pieces of soap in a mesh bag and hang it to an outdoor faucet for a quick wash-up.

Irmgard Haskins
Garberville, CA

Beat the Itch

A homemade remedy for poison ivy, oak and sumac is to mix equal parts vinegar and rubbing alcohol and apply it to the rash.

Mary Ann Marino
West Pittsburgh, PA

Editor's Tip

Here's a simple, two-in-one, reusable tool: Cut a section of 1-inch-mesh hardware cloth (not chicken wire) about 24 by 36 inches. Fold the outer 4 inches, all around, at a 90-degree angle so you have what looks like a wire tray. Snip the corners and connect the cut ends of the wire for a tighter fit. Use this tool for sifting soil, compost or other loose gardening material. It also comes in handy if you want to keep cats, chipmunks, birds or other critters out of a small bed of seeds or seedlings, so you might want to make several at once.

A Gardening Glossary

Acid soil Any soil with a pH reading below 7.0 on a scale of 1 to 14; the lower the reading, the more acid the soil. Most garden plants prefer slightly acid to neutral soil. See pH.

Alkaline soil Any soil with a pH reading above 7.0 on a scale of 1 to 14; the higher the reading, the more alkaline the soil. See pH.

Annual A plant that completes its entire life cycle in one season.

Aphid A small sucking insect, usually pale green, gray or black. They are small and pear shaped, and appear in great numbers on young plant growth. You can recognize them by the fact that they secrete a sticky fluid called honeydew, which also attracts ants. Control aphids by knocking them off the plants with a hard stream of cold water or by spraying with insecticidal soap.

Bacillus thuringiensis (Bt) A species of bacteria that attacks caterpillars. Some kinds attack other pests, such as Japanese beetles and grasshoppers.

Beneficial insects Insects that help rather than hinder gardening efforts. They might pollinate, eat harmful insects, or may breakdown plant material in the soil and release nutrients.

Biennial A plant that takes two years to complete its life cycle, growing leafy growth the first season, then flowering in its second season before dying.

Bolting The formation of flowering stalks, especially on plants grown for their leaves or roots, lowering harvest quality.

Borer A pest that bores into the stems of plants, usually a larva such as a grub, caterpillar or maggot. Symptoms often include an entrance hole and wilt on stem portions beyond. They can be controlled by digging out the pest, injecting an appropriate botanical or microbial insecticide, or by pruning the plant below the damage and destroying it with the pest.

Bulb An underground part of the plant that stores energy. It is made of layers of fleshy and dried leaf bases and has roots attached to its bottom.

Bulbil Small bulb-like organs attached to a plant. Underground it's called a bulblet.

Climber A vine that climbs on its own, using twining, gripping pads, tendrils or some other method of attaching itself to structures or other plants.

Companion planting Intermixing different crops to benefit one or more of them. Some people plant roses and chives together, for example.

Compost Decayed organic matter that looks like soil. It is used to improve the texture and fertility of garden soil.

Corm A bulb-like, underground storage structure. Crocuses and gladioli grow from corms.

Cover crop A crop grown to occupy or improve the soil in a part of the garden that is not currently producing.

Crop rotation Planting different kinds of plants in the same spot over different years. It helps balance soil nutrients and slows the cycle of pests and diseases.

Cross-pollination When one plant pollinates another, different plant. The seeds will grow into a plant that looks different from the parents.

Crown The base of a plant, where stem and bud join; usually but not always at ground level. Many perennials grow from crowns.

Cutting Removing a part of a stem or root so it can develop into a new plant.

Cutworm The caterpillar of several kinds of moths. They emerge from the soil at night and "cut down" seedlings, then devour them, leaving no evidence beyond the severed stem. To stop them, try putting 1-inch-tall collars around the stem of newly set transplants so that the cutworms can't get to them.

Damping off A group of fungal diseases that attack seedlings and make the stem wither at the soil line, causing the plant to topple over. There is no cure for affected plants, but you can prevent the disease by growing the seedlings in a warm, bright, airy location. Avoid overwatering, too.

Division Breaking or cutting apart of the crown of a plant to make additional plants.

Espalier Growing trees supported by structures, to form a narrow hedge or fence. Espaliers are often trained to grow flat along the south face of a stone or brick wall which holds heat overnight, making the fruit mature early.

Fertilizer Any material containing good amounts of plant nutrients, especially nitrogen (N), phosphorus (P) and potassium (K—also called potash). Fertilizers are required to have the analysis of these three nutrients printed on the container.

Fungicide Any material capable of killing fungi. Sulfur and copper sulfate are two common fungicides.

Germination The sprouting stage of a seed.

Green manure A crop grown only so you can turn it into the soil. This improves the soil by adding organic matter.

Hardening off The process of gradually exposing seedlings started indoors to outdoor conditions before transplanting.

Herbaceous A plant that dies to the ground in winter.

Herbicide A material that kills plants, generally weeds. Some soaps have herbicidal properties.

Humidity The amount of water in the air. Most houseplants like high humidity.

Hybrid A plant grown from seed crossed from two distinctly different plants.

Insecticidal soap Specially formulated soap that kills an insect, but is relatively harmless to plants.

Insecticide A material that kills insects. There are numerous powders that are toxic to insects, as well as biodegradable chemicals such as soaps.

Interplanting Mixing several different plants in the same planting space. You can do this for aesthetic reasons, pest and disease control or simply to raise the yield per square foot. See also Companion planting.

Latin name The scientific name of a plant. The Latin or botanical name consists of two parts: the genus name, which states the genus to which the plant belongs; and the species name, which describes the species to which the plant belongs.

Lime A rock powder that is used to raise the pH (that is, to decrease the acidity) of soils.

Maturity, days to For plants generally started indoors, the number of days from setting of transplants in the open garden until the first harvest. For crops sown directly in the garden, the number of days from seedling emergence to the first harvest.

Mealybug An insect that sucks plant juices. It covers itself in a white, cottony substance.

Nitrogen A major plant nutrient that's important for plant foliage.

NPK Initials for the three major plant nutrients contained in manure, compost and fertilizers. N is for nitrogen, P for phosphorus, and K for potassium.

Nutrient Any mineral that's essential for plant growth.

Nutrient deficiency When plants don't do well because they don't have enough of a particular nutrient. Yellowish leaves are often a symptom.

Organic matter That portion of the soil or plant material composed of living, or once living, organisms or their remains.

Parterre A kind of formal garden design wherein geometrically arranged beds are planted with edgings and decorative arranged crops, whether ornamental or edible, or both. See also Potager.

Pathogen Anything that causes a plant disease.

Peat Partially decomposed mosses and sedges harvested from bogs and used as a component of soil-less potting mixes.

Peat pots Planting pots made from compressed peat. These are used for plants that don't like to be disturbed because the young plants roots will grow through the walls of the pot.

Perennial Any plant that lives more than three years. Perennials can be herbaceous or woody.

Perlite A white, porous material that is used to improve the drainage of potting mixes. See also Vermiculite.

pH A symbol for the acid-alkaline balance of the soil. The balance is expressed as a number from 1 to 14, with 7 considered neutral. A pH of 6 is acidic while a pH of 8 is alkaline. Higher numbers are more alkaline, lower numbers more acidic.

Phosphorus A major plant nutrient. Phosphorus is often associated with flowering.

Potager A French term applied to food gardens that are decorative as well as functional. See also Parterre.

Potassium A major plant nutrient associated with the strength of roots and stems.

Pruning The removal of plant parts to improve the health, appearance or productivity of the plant.

Rhizome A horizontal stem, usually underground, from which grow both leaves and roots. Usually persistent from year to year. Tall bearded iris grow from rhizomes.

Rootbound A situation where plant roots have filled the container where they grow. Plants that are highly rootbound quit growing.

Slug A snail-like creature that eats plant parts. It crawls along the soil and leaves slimy trails behind it.

Soil-less mix Any potting mix that is made without soil. Some common components include peat, bark, coconut fiber, vermiculite, perlite and sand.

Succession planting Replanting a crop at intervals throughout the growing season to get longer harvest.

Topdressing Applying fertilizer to the surface of the soil around established plantings.

Tuber An underground plant part that stores nutrients. It can either be part of the stem or the roots. Stem tubers make buds on their surface where shoots may grow from the following season; root tubers sprout from the point at which they were attached to the stem of the parent plant. Dahlias and potatoes are tubers.

Vermiculite A gray, mica-like material that is used to improve the drainage of potting mixes. See also Perlite.

Whitefly A white, fly-like insect that sucks the juices from plants.

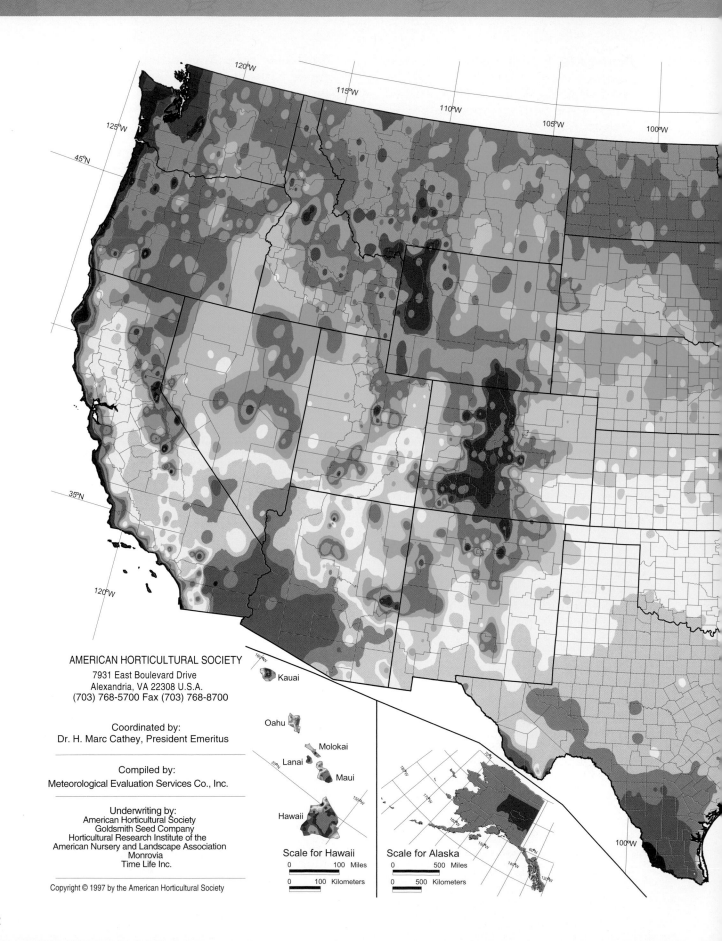

AMERICAN HORTICULTURAL SOCIETY

7931 East Boulevard Drive
Alexandria, VA 22308 U.S.A.
(703) 768-5700 Fax (703) 768-8700

Coordinated by:
Dr. H. Marc Cathey, President Emeritus

Compiled by:
Meteorological Evaluation Services Co., Inc.

Underwriting by:
American Horticultural Society
Goldsmith Seed Company
Horticultural Research Institute of the
American Nursery and Landscape Association
Monrovia
Time Life Inc.

Kauai

Oahu

Molokai

Lanai

Maui

Hawaii

Scale for Hawaii

0		100 Miles
0		100 Kilometers

Scale for Alaska

0		500 Miles
0		500 Kilometers

American Horticultural Society Plant Heat-Zone Map

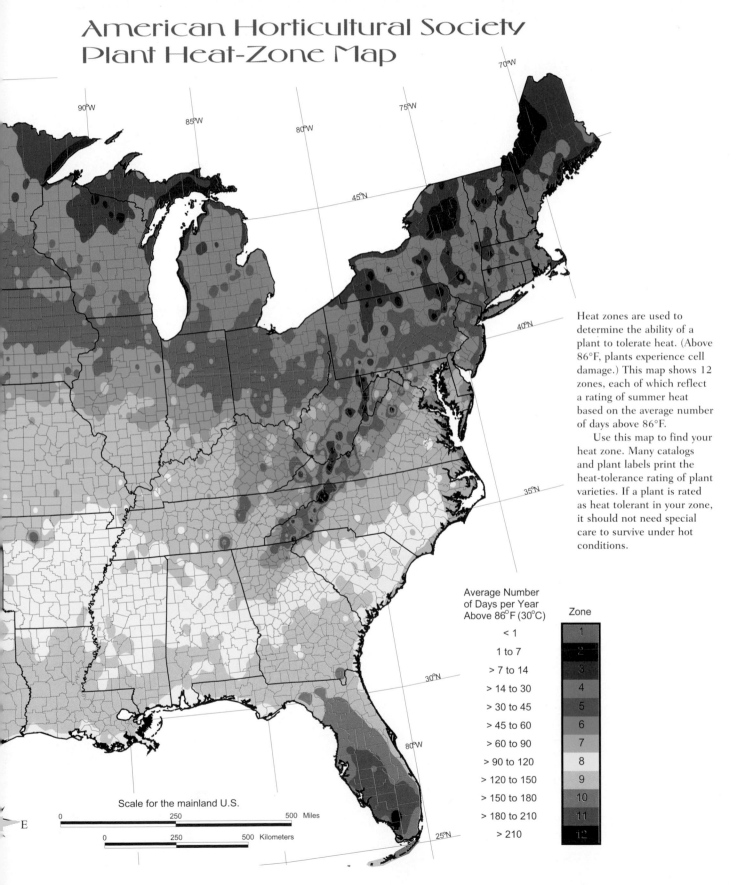

Heat zones are used to determine the ability of a plant to tolerate heat. (Above 86°F, plants experience cell damage.) This map shows 12 zones, each of which reflect a rating of summer heat based on the average number of days above 86°F.

Use this map to find your heat zone. Many catalogs and plant labels print the heat-tolerance rating of plant varieties. If a plant is rated as heat tolerant in your zone, it should not need special care to survive under hot conditions.

Average Number of Days per Year Above 86°F (30°C)	Zone
< 1	1
1 to 7	2
> 7 to 14	3
> 14 to 30	4
> 30 to 45	5
> 45 to 60	6
> 60 to 90	7
> 90 to 120	8
> 120 to 150	9
> 150 to 180	10
> 180 to 210	11
> 210	12

Scale for the mainland U.S.

0   250   500 Miles

0   250   500 Kilometers

Average Dates of First Fall Frost

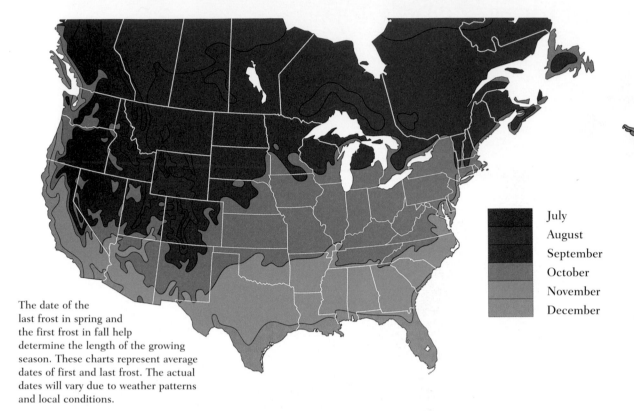

	July
	August
	September
	October
	November
	December

The date of the last frost in spring and the first frost in fall help determine the length of the growing season. These charts represent average dates of first and last frost. The actual dates will vary due to weather patterns and local conditions.

Average Dates of Last Spring Frost

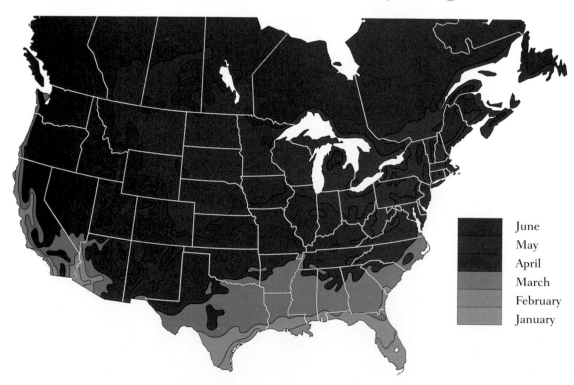

	June
	May
	April
	March
	February
	January

USDA Plant Hardiness-Zone Map

The USDA Hardiness Zone map separates the country into zones with similar growing conditions based on average minimum temperatures.

Look for Zone ratings on plant labels and in catalogs to help you select plants that will overwinter in your area.

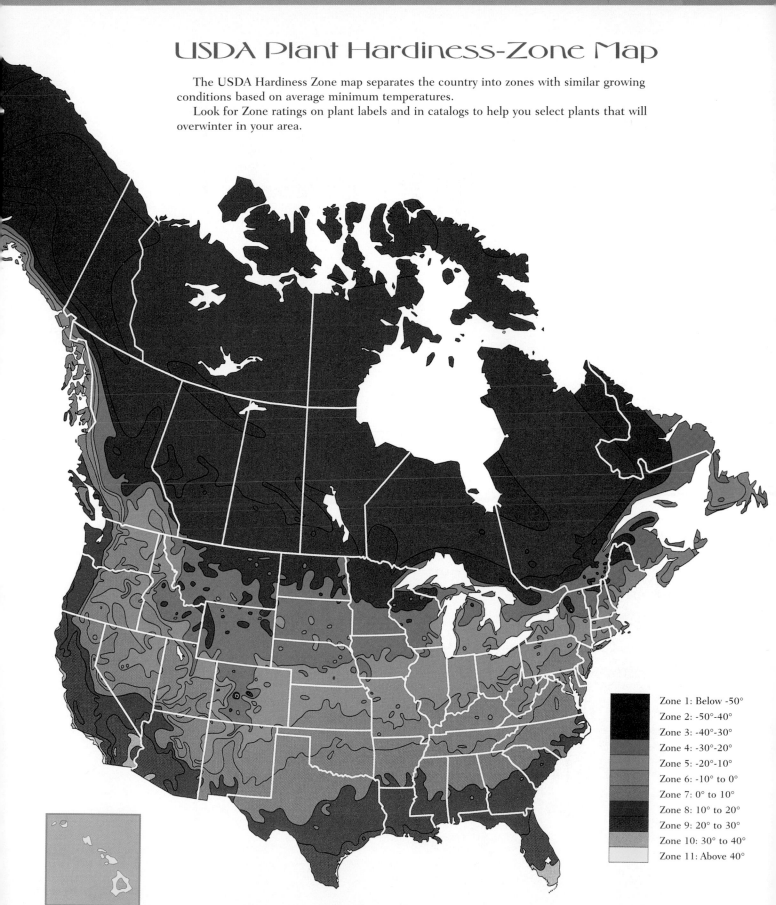

Zone 1: Below -50°
Zone 2: -50°-40°
Zone 3: -40°-30°
Zone 4: -30°-20°
Zone 5: -20°-10°
Zone 6: -10° to 0°
Zone 7: 0° to 10°
Zone 8: 10° to 20°
Zone 9: 20° to 30°
Zone 10: 30° to 40°
Zone 11: Above 40°

Sources for Plants, Seeds and Supplies

VEGETABLE AND FLOWER SEEDS

Burpee Seeds
300 Park Avenue
Warminster, PA 18974
800-888-1447

Cook's Garden
P.O. Box 535
Londonderry, VT 05148
802-824-3400

Johnny's Selected Seeds
Foss Hill Road
Albion, ME 04910
207-437-4301

Nichols Garden Nursery
1190 North Pacific
Hwy.
Albany, OR 97321
541-928-9280

Park Seed
1 Parkton Ave.
Greenwood, SC 29647
800-845-3369

Pinetree Garden Seeds
P.O. Box 300
New Gloucester, ME
04260
207-926-3400

Shepherd's Garden
Seeds
30 Irene St.
Torrington, CT 06790
860-482-3638

PERENNIALS AND SHRUBS

Bluestone Perennials
7213 Middle Ridge Rd.
Madison, OH 44057
800-852-5243

Carroll Gardens
444 E. Main St.
Westminster, MD 21157
800-638-6334
Joy Creek Nursery
20300 N.W. Watson
Road
Scappoose, OR 97056
503-543-7474

Klehm Nursery
4210 N. Duncan Rd.
Champaign, IL 61821
800-553-3715

Milaeger's Gardens
4838 Douglas Ave.
Racine, WI 53402
800-669-9956

Niche Gardens
111 Dawson Road
Chapel Hill, NC 27516
919-967-0078

Siskiyou Rare Plant
Nursery
2825 Cummings Road
Medford, OR 97501
503-772-6846

Andre Viette Nursery
Rt. 1, Box 16
Fishersville, VA 22939
703-942-2118

Wayside Gardens
1 Garden Lane
Hodges, SC 26965
800-845-1124

White Flower Farm
P.O. Box 50
Litchfield, CT 06759
800-503-9624

Woodlanders
1128 Colleton Ave.
Aiken, SC 28901
803-648-7522

BULBS

Dutch Gardens
P.O. Box 200
Adelphia, NJ 07710
800-818-3861

McClure & Zimmerman
P.O. Box 368
Friesland, WI 53935
414-326-4220

Van Bourgondien
P.O. Box 1000
Babylon, NY 11702
800-622-9997

ROSES

Antique Rose Emporium
Rt. 5, Box 143
Brenham, TX 77833
409-836-9051

Jackson & Perkins
P.O. Box 1028
Medford, OR 97501
800-292-4769

Royall River Roses
70 New Gloucester Rd.
North Yarmouth, ME
04097
800-820-5830

HERBS

Mountain Valley
Growers
38325 Pepperweed Rd.
Squaw Valley, CA 93675
209-338-2775

Sandy Mush Herb
Nursery
316 Surrett Cove Rd.
Leicester, NC 28748
704-683-2014

Sunnybrook Farms
9448 Mayfield Rd.
P.O. Box 6
Chesterland, OH 44026
216-729-7232

FRUITS

Northwoods Nursery
27635 S. Oglesby Rd.
Canby, OR 97013
503-266-5432

Raintree Nursery
391 Butts Rd.
Morton, WA 98356
360-496-6400

Stark Brothers
P.O. Box 10
Louisiana, MO 63353
800-325-4150

TROPICALS

Brudy's Exotics
P.O. Box 820874
Houston, TX
77282-0874
800-926-7333
Web Site Catalog:
http://www.brudys-exotics.com

Glasshouse Works
Church Street
Stewart, OH 45778
740-662-2142
Web Site Catalog:
http://www.glass-houseworks.com

Logee's Greenhouses
141 North Street
Danielson, CT 06239
203-774-8038

Stokes Tropicals
P.O. Box 9868
New Iberia, LA
70562-9868
800-624-9706
Web Site Catalog:
http://www.stokes-tropicals.com

SUPPLIES

Gardener's Supply Co.
128 Intervale Road
Burlington, VT 05041
800-234-6630

Gardens Alive!
5100 Schenley Place
Lawrenceburg, IN
47025
812-537-8650

Peaceful Valley Farm
Supply
P.O. Box 2209
Grass Valley, CA 95945
916-272-4769

Worm's Way
3151 S. Highway 446
Bloomington, IN 47401
800-274-9676

WATER GARDENING PLANTS AND EQUIPMENT

Lilypons Water Gardens
P.O. Box 10
Buckeystown, MD
21717
(also locations in Texas
and California)
800-723-7667

Perry's Water Gardens
1831 Leatherman
Gap Rd.
Franklin, NC 28734
704-369-2056

Index